W9-BYC-289

Looking
Forward

Looking *Forward*

Voices *from* Church Leaders *on Our* Global Mission

Compiled & edited by
Mission to the World
Presbyterian Church in America

Printed in the United States of America

Packaged by WinePress Publishing, PO Box 428, Enumclaw, WA 98022. The views expressed or implied in this work do not necessarily reflect those of WinePress Publishing. The author(s) is ultimately responsible for the design, content and editorial accuracy of this work.

ISBN 1-57921-500-9
Library of Congress Catalog Card Number: 2002112303

Acknowledgements
All of Grace—A Pilgrimage of Faith

It is thrilling to come to this point in the history of the Presbyterian Church in America and of Mission to the World when, for the first time in our denomination, we come together for a global missions conference. It is the occasion for the publication of this book.

I gratefully acknowledge those who made this book possible—in particular, the vision and direction of Bruce Terrell and the tireless and masterful editing of Marty Davis. I am indebted, as well, to all who contributed their thoughts to this volume; they made sacrifices of time and energy in the midst of very busy schedules.

At the beginning of our short history, we could not have envisioned how God would work in our midst. Could we have foreseen that the PCA would have more than seven hundred missionaries in forty-seven countries over the globe? Did we imagine the numbers of men, women, and children that God would call to Himself and the Church that He would establish? That God has blessed us so greatly requires that we once more affirm that it is all His gracious work. To the degree that He has chosen to bless our feeble and foolish efforts reflects, not only His gracious work in our lives, but also His desire to bless the nations. "God our God blesses us that all the ends of the earth may fear Him" (Ps. 67:1).

We also must acknowledge that we—in our own time—stand upon the shoulders of those who have gone before us. It would not be possible to tell the names of the many whose vision and wise planning gave us the foundation upon which we build. Nor could we ever adequately thank the ones who poured out their lives around the world representing Christ and His Church, many of whom went as pioneers in our fledgling mission efforts. They followed Christ, battled the evil one, and left a path for us to follow.

Equally significant, there are men, women, boys, and girls who sacrificed materially and labored in prayer and are also deserving of our heartfelt thanks. Most of these sacrifices were made in secret, unseen and unknown by the rest of us. Often they were costly. Even as others went to battle, these were the faithful who stayed with the baggage. And as we read in 1 Sam. 30:24: "And who will listen to you in this matter? For as his share is who goes down to the battle, so shall his share be who stays by the baggage; they shall share alike." Until eternity we will not know the value and importance of their work.

Finally, we remind ourselves that we are but pilgrims together. The story is not about us, but about Jesus who sought us when we were "strangers, wandering from the fold of God." It is about the grace of God to which we are indebted. And as we come together in thanksgiving and praise, we raise the Ebenezer of our own time and generation.

We must look back to remember what God has done and say, "thank you." We must raise our stone of remembrance. But the journey is not over. The great cloud of witnesses encourages us to run the race and to look to Jesus. Jesus beckons us forward. And in His name we go.

Paul D. Kooistra
Coordinator, Mission to the World
August 2002

Foreword

Listening to the evening news program on National Public Radio on my way home from work, I heard a humorous and interesting essay by a young man who had just run in the Boston Marathon. A friend of his who ran the marathon the previous year had recruited him to run. His friend was trained and ready. He, on the other hand, had not trained, and was completely unprepared.

Most of his narrative recounted humorous anecdotes like suffering the indignity of being overtaken at mile five by a man wearing a tuba to promote music education, and subsequently being surpassed by a seventy-year-old man at mile ten. He also described the painful reality of toenails that were bleeding and literally falling off during the course of the race because he did not wear the appropriate running shoes. At mile thirteen, he collapsed on the side of the road and urged his friend to go on without him to the finish line. His only consolation was making it at least as far as the twelve-mile mark where the hundreds of Wellesley girls had stationed themselves to cheer the runners on. Of course, in his mind they were there solely to support him in his gallant effort.

At the end of the essay the writer outlined two conclusions he had reached after reflecting on his experience: First, buy the right shoes. Second, have the right end in mind before running the race. Doesn't it always come back to the basics? The fundamentals. Our tendency, rather, is to so overly complicate and sophisticate that we lose the essentials in our lives and ministry.

I got the idea for this book shortly after hearing that essay. The question that came to my mind was are we getting it right? Are we losing the basics in our post-modern savvy? And what is the forum for our church, the PCA, to talk about this marathon we're running? This book is an attempt to do just that—to help us dialogue and not forget the basics. Just like the Boston Marathon participant, we need to wear the right shoes and head for the right goal.

But what are some of the basics in missions today? To what extent should our current global context influence our thinking? How are our strategies, decisions, and actions driven by the fact that we are early 21st century North American evangelical Presbyterians?

This book is not an attempt to offer conclusive answers to all the issues. There are numerous books, periodicals, websites, etc. that speak to the topics discussed in this book.

This book is, however, an effort to have the PCA talk with the PCA (and others who want to listen) about critical issues in global ministry today. We have begun to build a great heritage in our relatively young denomination to think and act globally. We want to educate and motivate ourselves to even greater commitment and involvement in our Lord's Great Commission. We hope the articles written by the numerous contributors from significantly different perspectives will spur further thinking and dialogue to that end. In short, we hope this book helps us run the race wearing the right shoes and having the right end in mind.

Bruce Terrell
Chief Operating Officer, MTW
July 2002

Contents

Section I—Fundamentals: Looking Deeper

Global Missions: Our Theological Foundations

Paul D. Kooistra

Reformed Theology

Mission to the World, as an arm of the Presbyterian Church in America, a confessional church, does Reformed and covenantal missions around the world. The Reformed faith, in its simplest definition, is God-centered faith. God alone is the source of all that exists and everything that exists does so for the glory of Him alone.

At the heart of what it means to be Reformed are the doctrines of grace. Central to these doctrines are the utter helplessness of man and the absolute trustworthiness of God. We should not forget that the doctrines of grace produce the virtues of the Christian life—love, humility, understanding and compassion. By emphasizing these Christian virtues as an important aspect of what it means to be Reformed we can develop a posture of being Reformed in theology and character in a warm and winsome way.

The great doctrine of sovereign grace, the truth that God saves men, is foundational to a theological understanding of missions. Neglect of this truth, which is found in the Scriptures and summarized in our confessional standards, cripples missions and reduces it to a human enterprise, seeking to "help" God. Missions is a divine enterprise, wherein God commands and graciously accepts the obedient participation of man. When people respond to the gospel, it is neither because of their responsiveness nor because of the obedience of the missionary that God finds them; it is because God found them that they are responsive. The truth that God chooses His people, some believe, discourages missions. On the contrary, this truth is the only real ground for missions.

The Reformed faith also teaches the finitude and sinfulness of our estate. It underlines our absolute dependence on the Spirit of God to bring regeneration to those we long to see embrace Christ. Nothing is more exciting than to see someone come to faith. When God is pleased to use us as His instruments to bring about new life in His people, we are well aware of the fact that it is God's Spirit alone that can bring regeneration, repentance, and faith to anyone.

We believe that man is totally depraved, that is, that he cannot produce any spiritual life that would move him toward God. We shall, therefore, marvel, first of all, far more in our own salvation, which is beyond our comprehension and which is fully a gracious act from a loving God. We also understand in a deeper way that disobedience characterizes every part of a culture—politics, art and social life as well as religious life. Total depravity underlines the importance of understanding a culture and all of its parts in order to bring the gospel to the people of that culture. We do not, however, put our faith in our strategic plans, but are open to what God will do with us and through us as His ambassadors.

We believe in unconditional election. We, therefore, look more to Christ and His gospel message for our mission activity and far less to our gifts that He has given us or to the environment in which we work.

We believe in limited atonement. We, therefore, have a far greater sense of belonging to God and believing that the One who created the universe also created us and saved us to be His kingdom instruments in this world. Rather than limiting our efforts to bring the gospel to others, acceptance of this truth compels us to scatter the seed wherever we can, believing that God has chosen His people in every tongue, tribe, and nation for whom He specifically came and died.

We believe in irresistible grace. We do not, therefore, run from those places where missionary activity seems very difficult. God calls some to plow in concrete and others to turn fertile soil that was prepared in the past by others. Reliance on His Spirit's guidance is an antidote to our fleshly desire only to concentrate our efforts where it is easy to plant churches and where we see a large response to the gospel.

We believe in the perseverance of the saints. Our activities, therefore, have a great measure of the joy of eternity and the everlasting fellowship we share with God. We entrust those whom God has brought to faith far more into His hands and less into our programs. We do not see the church as a fortress in which to hide, but rather a training school to send those whom God has brought to faith out into the world to continue His great redemptive plan.

Our commitment to Reformed theology is based on the fact that it is biblical. It is drawn from the heart of God to us, and without it there can be no lasting blessing from God. When we speak of the Reformed faith, we are talking about those truths of God and man, sin and grace, love and judgment, which find their basis in Scripture and which we as a denomination embrace in our *Westminster Confession of Faith* and its *Larger and Shorter Catechisms*.

The effects of sin are pervasive, and men and women are not only harmed by sin, they are dead in it. Many will not embrace the biblical doctrines of election, calling, and regeneration, but the evidence for the complete lostness of mankind, and therefore, the absolute necessity of these doctrines is everywhere. Our emphasis is one of full conviction that the doctrines of the Reformed faith are the truest expression of genuine biblical faith and what the world needs to hear. We shall stress a faith that grips all of life, and we shall encourage all stations in life as a sacred calling.

We will admit that there have been times when the Reformed faith has been held in an unloving and critical fashion. If we are going to build a Reformed church in the world, there must be within that movement a tolerance for diversity. We must resist going beyond Scripture and imposing our own definitions on what it means to be Reformed. We know that we do not have the final word on every issue.

Finally, the way our theology is applied and expressed is a measure of how biblical its content is. We hold firmly to our positions while embracing other godly men and women who disagree with us. Simply put, if the Reformed faith is biblical faith, then any theology that is not expressed in love is neither Reformed nor biblical!

Covenant Theology

To emphasize covenant theology is to emphasize the grace-conceived, grace-established and grace-perfected reality of the Church and its mission activity.

When God chose Israel, and therefore the Church, He did so for no reason that was conditional in or inherent in His people (Deuteronomy 7:7). The covenant established with Abraham in Genesis 15 was, in all of its outward manifestations, an ancient, Mideastern contract, but in fact it was not a typical transaction of that day. Only God passed through the aisle between the animals. In other words, God was saying, "I alone AM and can make this covenant with my people." If we can drink deeply from the truth of covenant theology, we shall be able to reorganize our priorities, so that the glory of God becomes the single most important passion in the life and work of the Church. The driving force of our ministry will not be a market-driven strategic plan, but rather the vision that God may be glorified among the people of all nations (Romans 1:5).

Seen from a covenant perspective, the doctrines of grace—especially election—are not viewed as a privileged position of safety from those who are lost, but rather a grace-centered relationship which empowers God's people to engage in mission service to the world. The arena of God's saving work is all of His creation. God has called His people by His covenant into a special relationship with Him in order to bring all of creation back from its broken state to its right relationship with God.

The Presbyterian Church in America, through its mission agency, Mission to the World, focuses on church planting because the Church is the corporate body that God has brought into being by His covenant. The saving work of God cannot be reduced to only a personalized salvation between God and individuals. It is within the covenant community of the church that we experience one of the most dynamic living realities of the power of Christ. As Lord of the Church, He lives within the corporate body as Prophet, Priest, and King. He is the God-Revealer, God-Savior and God-Ruler over His people.

Mission activity does not end with conversion. Our goal is always the establishment of a vibrant, worshiping community, the Church—a body of believers—that is able to reproduce itself through mission activity of its own, and one that is able to make a life-changing impact within the lost and fallen culture in which God has placed it.

The covenant God has made with His people always has a twofold purpose. God has called His people for worship, and that worship motivates the Church for ministry. We must avoid the temptation to focus internally only on nurture at the expense of ministry or vice versa. The life of the covenant community must always be balanced with the Church's responsibility for the needs of the world.

Who belongs to the covenant community of God? There is great debate on this matter within evangelical Christianity. We believe, however, that the teaching of Scripture on this matter is very clear. All who believe by faith alone on Christ for salvation and their children are participants in the covenant promises. We do not believe in baptismal regeneration or in presumptive regeneration. That is, we do not believe that because a child has been baptized, or because his parents are believers in Christ, the child is automatically a member of the elect of God. On the other hand, the covenant promises have always been for those who have believed and their children. This is true in the Old Testament (Genesis 17:7), and what is true in the Old Testament, we believe must be true in the New Testament. At no time does God say that He has changed the extent of the covenant although He does tell us that He has changed the sign. To remove the covenant promises from the children of believers would be to reduce the covenant in the New Testament when in fact the New Testament is the fullness or fulfillment of that which was first promised to Abraham.

The Covenant Commission of the Old Testament was that the people of God were to teach faithfully the commandments of God to their children at all times and in all experiences of life (Deuteronomy 6:6–8). The Covenant Commission of the New Testament is just as you would expect—an expansion or a fulfillment of the Commission in the Old Testament. The people of God are to reach out to the peoples of all nations, baptizing them into the church and teaching them to apply the commandments of God to all of life (Matthew 28:19–20).

Dr. Paul Kooistra *served as president of Covenant Theological Seminary from 1983–1994, and since that time has served the PCA as Coordinator of Mission to the World.*

World Mission and the Global City

TIM KELLER

The two great new realities for world mission are "urbanization" and "globalization."

Urbanization

A recent article in *The Economist* tells that in 1950 New York was the only world city with a population of over ten million people. Today there are over twenty such cities, twelve of which have arrived in the last two decades, with many more to come. All of these new mega-cities are developing in what used to be called the Third World. Why?

In the 18th century, a combination of population growth and technology brought rural Europe to its "carrying capacity," creating a surplus population, and in every family some left countryside and small towns to make a living elsewhere. As a result there were a hundred fifty years of urbanization in which the great cities of Europe swelled to be the largest in the world. Many experts now believe this is beginning to happen in Africa, Asia, and to a lesser extent in Latin America, where the cities are literally exploding with new immigrants from the villages and rural areas. If urban-rural population in the Southern Hemisphere stabilizes at 75%–25% as it did in Europe and North America, then over the next few decades we will see over half a billion people move into the cities of Africa and Asia alone—the equivalent of one new Bangkok (eight million people) being created *every two months.*[1]

Urbanization and the Mission of the Church

It is this urban explosion that has been the main vehicle, in the providence of God, for the most important new development in Christian history in centuries. While Christianity has declined in Europe and has only held its own (at best) in North America, it has been growing at many times the rate of the population in Africa, Asia, and Latin America. Now the majority of Christians live south of the equator. Christianity is growing more rapidly than any other faith, but the vast majority of believers will be neither white nor European nor Euro-American.[2] Why? It is because of the staggering growth in cities. The millions of new residents of these burgeoning cities have two characteristics that make them far more open to Christianity than they were before arriving. First, they are more open to new ideas and change in general, having been uprooted from traditional settings. Second, they have great need for help and support in order to face the moral, economic, emotional, and spiritual pressures of city life. The old kinship support networks of the rural areas are weak or absent, while the cities have "next to nothing in working government services."[3] Churches offer supportive community, a new spiritual family, and a liberating gospel message. "Rich pickings await any groups who can meet these needs of these new urbanites, anyone who can at once feed the body and nourish the soul."[4]

This is remarkably similar to the first great explosion of church growth and mission. In His providence, God also used urban settings and problems in the first centuries AD to be the vehicle for the first great expansion of the Christian church. The "mechanism" for the expansion was the same. First, urban dwellers are always more open to change and to new ideas because the city itself is a venue of constant change. Second, urban dwellers face more pressures and therefore are more prone to ask the big questions about meaning and hope, and are more in need of new community and support.

> *Christianity served as a revitalization movement that arose in response to the misery, chaos, fear, and brutality of life in the urban Greco-Roman world. . . . Christianity revitalized life in. . . .cities by providing new norms and new kinds of social relationships able to cope with many urgent urban problems. To cities filled with the homeless and the impoverished, Christianity offered charity as well as hope. To cities filled with newcomers and strangers, Christianity offered an immediate basis for attachments. To cities filled with orphans and widows, Christianity provided a new and expanded sense of family. To cities torn by violent ethnic strife, Christianity offered a new basis for social solidarity. And to cities faced with epidemics, fires, and earthquakes, Christianity offered effective . . . services.*[5]

Globalization

The technological/communication revolution has led to an unprecedented mobility of people, ideas, and capital, which is often called "globalization."

First, this means that major world cities are far more connected to other major cities around the world than they are to their own nations. On the one hand, the business-class and other elites of New York, London, and Tokyo are able to identify more with one another than with the non-urban citizens of their own countries.[6] But the strong connections between major cities are not only through the elite. Huge, diverse immigrant populations in global cities tie each urban area more tightly to scores of other countries around the world than to its own regional locale. In other words, thousands of residents of NYC are far more connected to the Philippines, Haiti, Columbia, China, and Nigeria then they are to New Jersey or Connecticut.

Second, these networked world-cities are becoming more economically and culturally powerful than the national governments of their geographical regions. Why is this? 1) The mobility of capital means national governments are now virtually powerless to control the flow of money in and out of their own economies, thus greatly decreasing their influence in general. The cities are the seats of multi-national corporations and international economic, social, and technological networks. 2) The technology/communication revolution means that national governments are powerless also to control what their people watch or learn. (This was a major factor in the collapse of communism in Europe.) As a result, it is the culture/values set of world-class cities that is now being transmitted around the globe to every tongue, tribe, people, and nation. A major city like New York or Los Angeles now is far more influential in forming the culture of residents in, say, rural Indiana or rural Mexico than are the national or local governments or civic institutions. Whereas power has for eight hundred years been centralized in the nation-state, we now are seeing the first overall major erosion of that power.

Harvie Conn concludes that we are witnessing again the rise of the City-State. He quotes N. Pierce: "Great metropolitan regions—not states, not even the nation-states—are starting to emerge as the world's most influential players" (p. 182). Thus, world-class cities are increasingly crucial to setting the course of culture and life as a whole, even in the areas of the world (Europe and North America) where cities are not literally growing in size.[7] In other words, urban culture now reaches out far beyond the city limits into the suburbs and even rural areas. Kids in Iowa or even Mexico are becoming more like young adults in L.A. and New York City than they are like adults in their own locales. The coming economic, social, and cultural world order will be a global, multicultural, urban order.

Global Cities and the Mission of the Church

What are the implications of these two trends for world mission?

First, *reach the city to reach the world.* In general, world missions should concentrate more on cities than on anywhere else. I think the evidence is overwhelming and obvious for this. This, of course, is no argument for neglecting any particular people group or part of the world. The church needs to minister the gospel wherever there are people! But many of the current unreached people groups in remote areas of the world may be gone within twenty years (into the cities!). The problem for the American church is that white evangelical Protestants who control the U.S. mission apparatus are themselves overwhelmingly non-urban in background. They neither understand nor like urban life and realities. But to the city we must go.

> *. . . "He determined the times set for them and* ***the exact places where they should live****. God did this so men would seek him and perhaps reach out for him and find him." . . . . God in our time is moving climactically through a variety of social, political, and economic factors to bring earth's peoples into closer contact with one another, into greater interaction and interdependence, and into earshot of the gospel. Through worldwide migration to the city God may be setting the stage for Christian mission's greatest and perhaps final hour . . . Now that a majority of the world's unreached populations live in cities, it is reasonable to expect that we will be redesigning . . . to address an urbanizing world in an accurate and balanced way. . . . To ignore the plight of the urban masses or refuse to grapple with the trials and complexities of city life is worse than merely a strategic error. It is unconscionable disobedience to God, whose providence directs the movements of people and creates special movements of missionary opportunity. The world of the twenty-first century will be urban, and so will Christian mission.* [8]

Second, *reach the city to reach both your region* **and** *"overseas."* The old distinction between home-missions and foreign-missions is made obsolete by global cities—and yet the city is more than ever the key to both! One urban church in Queens has planted three daughter churches: one in neighboring College Point, one in the neighboring Bronx, and one in the neighboring Philippines! Why? The church reached so many Filipino immigrants in its neighborhood that the new Christians wanted to plant a daughter church among their friends and relatives in their country of origin. Each major city is now a "portal" to most of the nations of the world. That is where they must be reached. But not only are cities the key to what used to be called "foreign missions," but they are the key to "home missions." You can't reach the urban centers from the suburbs, but you can most definitely reach the suburbs from the city. Regional people-flow is from the urban center outward. Students grow up, singles get married, immigrants make money and want more space—and all of them move out from the center to the suburbs. Ministries that begin and thrive in the city will eventually spread all through the suburbs, following their converts out to their new neighborhoods. But ministries that begin in the suburbs only reach inward toward the city center with great difficulty.

Third, *reach the city to reach the culture.* As we have seen, cities more than ever influence the culture and values of the world. The single most effective way for Christians to influence the culture of a nation is to have large numbers of them stay in cities and simply "be the church" there. Also, for all the reasons noted above, we would find increasingly that ministry which is effective in a world-class city has remarkably wide applicability, especially with the emerging generations.

Fourth, *reach the whole city to reach the world.* As we have seen, there is no part of the city that can be neglected. First, the poor cannot be neglected because God has always worked mightily among the urban poor. Word and deed ministry will have to be combined, both in ministries to Christians within the community and outside of it. The church's attitude toward and work with the poor will be a significant sign of its validity to others. Second, the immigrants—the nations—cannot be neglected, because they are far more open to (and more conscious of their need for) gospel ministry than they ever were in their homeland. Third, the elites cannot be neglected because they are disproportionately powerful and must be called to use their educational, economic, and cultural power for the service of others and the Lord.

Fifth, *reach the whole city to reach your own heart with the gospel.* In the city you'll find many things that will challenge your grasp of the gospel, many people that seem hopeless to you spiritually and morally. But if the gospel of grace is true, why would you think their conversion to be any more a miracle than your own? You will find people of other religions and of no religion who are wiser, kinder, and deeper than you. Even after growth in grace, lots of Christians are weaker people than lots of non-Christians. But if the gospel of grace is true, why *did* you think that Christians are basically better kinds of people than non-Christians? After a while these and other examples will begin to show you that, even though you may intellectually understand the doctrine of justification by faith alone, you functionally assume salvation by moral goodness and works. Ministry in the city, then, will help you grasp the gospel of grace in powerful ways. You may even come to see that you spiritually need the city more than the city needs you.

***Dr. Timothy Keller** is the founding pastor of Redeemer Presbyterian Church, New York City, and continues to serve that congregation as senior pastor.*

1. This assertion and everything in the preceding paragraph are taken from the *Economist* article "The Brown Revolution" (May 9, 2002).
2. Philip Jenkins, *The Next Christendom: The Coming of Global Christianity* (Oxford, 2002), p. 2.
3. Jenkins, p. 93.
4. Jenkins, p. 94.
5. Rodney Stark, *The Rise of Christianity* (Harper, 1996), p. 161.
6. See Saskia Sassen, *The Global City: New York, London, Tokyo* (Princeton U., 1991).
7. Harvie Conn, *The American City and the Evangelical Church* (Baker, 1994), pp. 181–182.
8. Roger Greenway, "World Urbanization and Missiological Education", in *Missiological Education for the Twenty-First Century: Essays in Honor of Paul Pierson* (Orbis, 1996).

The Tapestry of Contextualization

NELSON JENNINGS

"Contextualization" is one of those big words that most Christians think represents a good thing, even though they may be a bit unclear as to what it actually means. As a concept, contextualization is on the one hand quite simple and straightforward. However, its wider connections and ramifications—both practical and theoretical—are truly complex. The term itself has an interesting background, and unraveling its usage will help us pinpoint some of the nuances of this absolutely crucial missiological reality.

The Term

In North American English, the suffix "-ization" indicates an act, process or result of making or doing something; compare such familiar terms as "privatization," "realization" and "legalization." Insofar as contextualization is used in reference to the Christian faith, the term therefore means Christianity becoming "contextual," or appropriate and fitting to its various settings. All such settings for the Christian faith—including downtown Los Angeles, southern Sudan, and Brazilian footballers—have their own particular characteristics, so an almost equivalent term would be "particularization." Put simply, then, contextualization refers to the "particularization(s)" of the universal Christian faith into individual contexts or settings.

So far, so good. Note again that contextualization is an act, process, or result. For clarity's sake, for now at least, let's think of it as a *process*. To be sure, there are various parties engaged in the *act* of contextualization; we will come back to that later. One can also point to *resulting* contextualizations of the Christian faith, although such results are never final because of the dynamic character of the parties and contexts involved. It is better to think of such resulting contextualizations (or "expressions") of Christianity as snapshots of an ongoing process, whether it be Christian marriage in 21st-century America, articulations of the trinity in the ancient church creeds, worship in the late-19th-century Pacific Islands, 1980s leadership styles in Korean Presbyterian churches, or the churches' relationships with the state in contemporary Uganda.

As an actual word and focal point of discussion, "contextualization" was coined in the early 1970s. At the time the term was intended to draw attention to the socio-politico-economic aspects of any situation or context in which the gospel was at work. This was due to the fact that during the 1960s the collective worldwide Church, and missiologists in particular, had become enamored with "indigenization" and its more narrow anthropological focus on such cultural realities as language and traditional customs. Evangelicals, who moved towards consolidating their worldwide identity at Lausanne in 1974, already had concerns about the growing influence of liberation theology and its emphasis on salvation in political and economic terms. Even so, prominent Third World evangelicals from Latin America, Africa and Asia pointed out the full scope of the Christian gospel, so most evangelicals have now accepted to one degree or another the need for the Christian faith in its entirety to be expressed in ways appropriate to each particular overall *context*.

The Agents

How one understands the process of contextualization depends in large part on who the primary agents of contextualization are understood to be, a factor noted earlier. One powerful North American evangelical instinct points to the expatriate (subconsciously assumed to be North American) missionary as the one primarily responsible to make the necessary adjustments to the form of the unchanging Christian message he or she brings, as well as to the resulting believers' lives and practices. After all, this instinct claims, compared to the receivers—who almost always are from non-Christian backgrounds—it is the missionary who not only knows the Bible, but also comes from a culture with a Christian heritage. By this scheme, the task of contextualization is daunting to be sure: the missionary has to communicate biblical truths given in ancient cultural forms to a totally different and non-Christian culture, all the while having to resist the temptation to import his or her own, altogether different cultural norms. Those in the receiving culture help the missionary learn their culture, and God somehow superintends the process, but the idea is that the expatriate Christian emissaries are primarily responsible for contextualizing the faith.

There are at least three reasons, however, why this instinct needs correction. First, it is out of date. That fact alone does not invalidate the concept, but viewing the expatriate missionary as primary is continuous with the pre-World War II image of how missions proceeded from "the West to the rest." Second, and speaking directly to the matter, God and the receiving agents are primary, not the expatriate emissary. The missionary (of whatever cultural background) is essential to bring the gospel to those settings that have not yet heard it. However, what is of basic importance is God's initiative in communicating to people in their own languages and contexts. He speaks, and people hear in their heart languages, and it is the dynamic communication process—contextualization—that occurs between God and indigenous people that is primary. That dynamic makes the missionary more like a third-party catalyst. Third, placing the missionary at the center of the contextualizing process tends to downplay the contextualized, particular character of the Christianity that he or she embodies and represents. The truth is that all expressions of the Christian faith bear the marks of their contexts. Moreover, no Christians embody the final and universal form of the faith, nor do any of us enjoy a vantage point outside of contextual realities that can dictate to others what is complete and normative.

Translatability

Some evangelicals will start to feel a bit queasy at this juncture, so at this tricky point we need to consider Christianity's basic trait of cultural and contextual *translatability*. God as Creator is wholly separate from His creation: He is transcendent. Yet God has remained involved with His fallen creation, preeminently through entering the world as a concrete man, becoming particularized or contextualized as Jesus of Nazareth. At the same time, God's Word, which centers and focuses on Jesus, speaks to all people in their particular languages as the Bible is (re-)translated again and again into new (and changing) languages. Jesus, thus, comes close to all kinds of people, to every tribe, tongue and nation. He is not a provincial or tribal Savior, but He is the covenant Lord and Redeemer of all the earth. Together with His translated Word, Jesus crosses over cultural and generational boundaries and enters new contexts, shouldering His way into the beliefs of all kinds of people. Unlike Islam, for example, which brings into alien settings an enduring Arabic Qur'an and foundation of life, Jesus and His Word are translated into ever new settings, whereby people come to worship and follow Him within the terms and contours of their own languages and contexts.[1]

Putting this translation process in a more explicitly theological way, the triune God speaks to particular people in their own mother tongues by His Word and Spirit, as well as through His emissaries. Because this God speaks in people's particular languages—whether English, Hebrew, Greek, Swahili, or any other human language—He shows Himself to be their/our God as well as the God of all peoples, not some foreign tribal deity. He transforms peoples and their settings from the inside out, so to speak.[2] To put it from a Christian perspective, since this God speaks our language and knows us intimately, He knows our past, pre-Christian heritage as well. We, and all other peoples, have always been responsible to this Creator, Covenant Lord. Our sin has been blinding us, the evil one has been deceiving us, but God has been wooing us to grope for Him and His truth. Now that He has brought or translated the good news of Jesus into our context, He is guiding the whole contextualizing process in which He grants faith and growth, shaping our understanding of the Christian faith and reforming our lives into Christlikeness.

Inherent to this translatability of God's living and written Word is a tension between the universality and particularity, or "contextuality," of the Christian faith. On the one hand there is one Lord, one faith, one baptism for Christianity. It is the same God who is the God of all His people around the world and down through the centuries. In tension, however, with this universalizing side of Christianity is the homing drive of the faith, the push towards being *our* faith in *our* God in *our* particular language within *our* setting. God's universality and transcendence help protect such a homing instinct from overly domesticating (yet another almost equivalent term for contextualizing) the faith into a syncretistic alliance with local particularities to a point of rendering Christian distinctives unrecognizable. In that sense, the Christian faith should always have a pilgrim character to it, such that it maintains a measure of counter-cultural teaching and practice. On the other hand, God's immanence in particular contexts—supremely exemplified in the Incarnation—helps protect the inherent transcultural, universal side of the Christian faith from making it foreign and irrelevant to, or quarantined away from, any facet of any particular context. This need for relevance and applicability is why contextualization is such an absolutely crucial missiological reality, as stated at the outset. A healthy contextualization cultivates a prophetic involvement of God's people within their particular contexts, avoiding the twin extremes of irrelevant quarantine and syncretistic localization.[3]

Redemption Applied

It is important to note as well, that this universal-particular, transculturalization-contextualization dynamic is not something just for settings where Christianity is relatively new. For an English-speaking, early 21st-century, North American context, that means that the "missiological" reality of contextualization is always taking place here as well, not just on the (foreign) field. Whereas pioneer, unreached sectors of the world's peoples have their own unique place in what "missions" involves, insofar as God's world mission is intent on comprehensively redeeming all of the earth, the mission field is still everywhere, including here. Full redemption of any and all contexts will only come at the eschaton, so contextualization will continue to be an ongoing reality in whatever setting the Lord's people find themselves.

Full redemption of the entire world and its particular contexts—worked out in ongoing processes of contextualization—involves a spectrum of dimensions of belief and practice: worldview, cognition, linguistic forms, behavior, communication, social structure, and decision-making processes.[4] How the Christian faith looks in each of these interrelated dimensions will of course vary from context to context—although the variance will not go beyond recognition of a common Christian identity. Thus, for example, a Christian worldview will include, among other marks, God as Creator, the ultimate place of Jesus of Nazareth and the central role in the world of the Holy Spirit. It becomes problematic, however, to speak of *the* Christian worldview, since worldviews are always to be found among particular Christians in particular contexts—including biblical worldviews. The same universal-particular dynamic is true of other dimensions of faith and practice as well. Thus, while Christian decision-making is to exemplify Spirit-led mutual submission, to speak of *the* Christian decision-making process moves into the danger area of making universally normative a particular, contextual reality.

A Closing Image

The manifestations of God's redemption throughout the earth and world history are like countless braids interwoven in one grand tapestry. Each braid has three strands: *sanctification* of God's people wrought by the Holy Spirit, the corresponding *discipleship* of God's people as they follow Jesus' example and teachings, and the *contextualization* of the covenant community's sanctified obedience in particular situations. The strands must not be unraveled away from each other, lest the entire tapestry become skewed and unbalanced. God is ever working among His people throughout the entire earth. How we concretely and contextually manifest our obedience to His gracious covenantal dealings with us is part of the worldwide venture of faith, guided by His Word and Spirit.

Rev. Nelson Jennings and his wife, Kathy, are former MTW missionaries to Japan. He is now assistant professor of missions at Covenant Theological Seminary.

1. Andrew Walls has pioneered much of current thinking and research into the translatability of the Christian faith, e.g., in his *The Missionary Movement in Christian History: Studies in the Transmission of Faith* (Maryknoll, New York: Orbis Books, 1996).
2. Kwame Bediako has explored this transforming and interpretative role of mother-tongue Scripture within each cultural context in, for example, "Gospel and Culture: Guest Editorial" *Journal of African Christian Thought* 2, 2 (December, 1999): 1.
3. I have borrowed this scheme from Lamin Sanneh, *Translating the Message: The Missionary Impact on Culture* (Maryknoll, New York: Orbis Books, 1989, pp. 39–46).
4. David Hesselgrave, "Contextualization that is Authentic and Relevant" *International Journal of Frontier Missions* 12, 3 (July–Sept., 1995): 116ff.

How Well Will the Church Minister After We Leave? Pursuing Sustainable Ministry

Paul Meiners

The building where the church met, like their own simple houses, was not that impressive—until you realized they had built so much of it with their own resources. As the pastor and leaders showed us around, you could see pride on their faces. Each one who spoke described construction or ministry that was fulfilling their vision. The pastor said little, but deferred to those he had "equipped for the work of ministry." They introduced members each of them were training in ministries in this poor community—like caring for the sick, training people in skills to earn a living, and using these as opportunities to tell others the gospel and encourage new believers. When we asked them how we could help, this seemed an unanticipated question. Over tea in the office, they came up with some small, hands-on projects in which we could work along side them, adding some value to on-going ministries of their church. This church is *sustainable,* we agreed—our help might enhance their ministry, but they know what they are doing and can prosper on their own. In fact, there is much we can learn from them!

We have a great goal to pursue—to use our involvement with churches and ministries in the rest of the world to stimulate their effectiveness, using their own God-given resources in ministering to their community—in a word—*sustainable*. The opposite is dependence on outside resources to carry on their work. In pursuing this goal, we will be encouraged by their obedience to the gospel to be even more effective in our own ministries in our communities in the Western world.

God Equips Each Church for Its Ministry

The Judean church in the New Testament had a long spiritual background, while the newer Gentile churches had more material security. Paul pointed out the importance of the church in Corinth contributing to the needs of the poorer church in Judea. Their gift would result in thanks that they had genuinely obeyed the gospel (2 Cor. 9:12–14) and were now in fellowship with the earlier, Judean, believers. Like spiritual gifts, God distributes resources differently so that we function as an interdependent body. We are to give according to what we *have,* not bemoan what we *don't have* (2 Cor 8:13–14; Ro 15:26–27). If one part of the body neglects the resources God gave them, believing they can only serve God if they had different resources, they show lack of faith in themselves, but even more lack of faith in God, since, "my God will meet all your needs" (Phil. 4:11–13,19; 2 Cor. 9:8–11).

How Has God Blessed Us Differently?

Often we don't understand the healthy way in which the Church around the world should interact with its other parts. It is too easy for us, as Westerners, to compare our resources to those of churches in the majority of the world, and conclude that we have most of the resources and they have few. Americans like to be helpers. Standing on our own, giving instead of asking for help, and finding our own creative solutions are all highly rated American values. Besides, poverty makes us feel guilty and uncomfortable. Two-Thirds World churches belong to cultures that value fitting into your community more than independence, helping each other out in times of need. Giving gifts is important if you have the means, and expressing your need is quite acceptable. Therefore it is natural for an American church to conclude, "We have the resources to help," and their sister church in another country to agree, "We have needs you can meet."

On closer look, what are some different resources with which God has equipped a Western church and her sister church in a poorer country? The chart below is a simplification, but should help us compare how they might partner in the poorer, host church's community.

Western Church Qualities	Host Church Qualities
More training in theology & ministry	Good memory and reality of faith
Communicate best in their own culture	Communicate best in their own culture
More economic resources, how to use them	Understand poverty, how to make do
Work better on quick results	Work better on long-term results
Develop big plans and strategies	Focus on consistently doing the basic things
Work for short time (2 weeks to 20 years)	Will be there before and after foreigners visit
Limited language skills	Fluent in multiple local languages
Attract attention in the local community	Fit into the local community
Don't know local culture	Understand local culture

Can Western Generosity Create Problems?

Western resources become a problem when we come as outsiders and become a temporary (up to twenty years) part of a church's community. As visitors we want to contribute, and to us the needs are obvious. So we organize, teach, pay the expenses, and leave resources behind. Here are some of the problems an overwhelming foreign impact can cause:

- Our resources influence decision-making. "He who pays the piper calls the tune."
- Other cultures have a strong sense of hospitality and like to please their guests. They defer to our decisions and won't offend us with what we'd call "honesty."
- By having significant impact as outsiders we become their "temporary community," and disturb their local community relationships. This shift in community alignment is harder

for us to understand because the majority of our suburban churches don't have such strong connections to their own communities.

- The church we help may decrease their efforts to creatively maximize their own resources by shifting their interest to using ours. Instead of planning ministry based on community opportunities, needs, and resources, their ministry plans reflect the goals and methods of their donors.

Let's illustrate with some ways ministry methods can change if a Western church takes a directing role through their generosity.

Reliance on Outside Resources	Reliance on Local Resources
Pastoral encouragement *focuses* on an annual conference with outside speakers enabled by outside money.	Pastoral encouragement *focuses* on monthly meetings of pastors in which they encourage each other.
Caring for the sick is mainly the time a medical team comes to work with the church, with thoughts of building a clinic and hiring a nurse (with outside support).	Caring for the sick is done by people in the church trained in community health, who visit people and help some see local medical staff with whom the church has relationships.
The church builds a building with outside money. They have not given much, since the foreign church was quite generous. Some years later it has deteriorated because the church can't afford to maintain it and few have the skills to fix that type of facility. They have contacted the donor church requesting funds for repairs.	The church builds a building, relying on their own money, materials and labor. Proud of their accomplishment and the camaraderie of their effort, they are excited to invite others to worship with them. When it's too full for the growth, they are able to use their own resources to expand it.

Does this mean that Western Christians should leave churches in other cultures alone? No, that would be disobedient to the missionary call and ignore the interdependence and global use of our gifts from God. The question is not "if", but "how" our efforts will promote sustainability instead of dependence. The key word in the comparison above is "reliance."

Here is our purpose—*It is our desire that believers carry on the ministry to which God has called them in their own environment by relying on the resources that are in their own hands. There are stages in their development toward maturity in their ministry when carefully used help of various forms from the outside will be a stimulus to their growth and equipping, but we believe that help should be temporary and nurture strength and independence, not create dependence.*

How Can We Purse Sustainability?

We can lay down some principles to follow in three important areas.

Turning Ministry Over to the Local Community

- Assume that in the near future you may be removed from your work. What can you do to be as dispensable as possible on that day?
- Training, not big classes with Amerian material, but relational mentoring is a key means of developing sustainability. From the very start ask this question: "Why am I doing this myself? If this activity pertains to the future of the body here, I should always be working with someone in order to train them to take it over!"
- Donors all want to be needed, think we have much to offer, and are tempted to make ourselves needed longer than necessary. We have to pursue these relationships as partnerships, promote the value added by the local community, and not perpetuate our role any more than is essential.
- Decisions should be made within community as much as possible. The greater our distance from the local community and culture, the less qualified we are to make good long-term decisions. Connect with groups of local leaders, be quiet, patient (for years!), and learn to listen. Develop church and ministry structures of multiple local leaders.
- Realize that the most effective lessons of governance are the ones you model, not those found in an organizational document that seems foreign to your national coworkers. Model open, accountable, mutual decisions in which there is "subjection to the brethren."

Ensuring Any Ministry Is Community Based

- Before committing to a new aspect of your work ask, "Can this be carried on from within the community?" If the answer is, "no" or "doubtful," then modify it, drop it, or make sure it is only temporary. If you believe it is important, test the community's interest, ability and commitment. If they don't provide key support, postpone it until it is appropriate to test it again.
- It's better to start small and respond to community interest and vision. To build vision is more valuable than to build structures. When their vision is adequate, they can build the appropriate structure.
- Beware the temptation to "improve" things by adding features that cannot be sustained with local resources. Such features can change a project from short-term "partnership" to long-term "paternalship." By adding surgery to a clinic you can lose the clinic. Shallow wells can be sustained, deeper ones will produce no water because the pump can't be maintained.
- Outside resources, when used, should be for new projects, ideas that are generated and designed by local leadership, projects of limited time and scope, and should act to stimulate local resources rather than replace or squelch them.
- Even if more of the resources come from outside, community resources must be key for the project to go ahead. Their resources may be primarily planning, "sweat equity" (labor), getting permissions, or generating community involvement. Whatever they provide, they must be able to say honestly "it couldn't have happened without us," and have ownership pride in the project. They must feel this is "our project", not "their project."
- Even using outside resources, it is still all about the local project, not about the outsider. The project should be designed to meet local needs and standards, not satisfy donor wishes. Key to this is that the primary decision-making needs to be close to the community. If there are not yet community people capable of making the decisions, the first step is to develop them, not bring in resources.

Avoiding Problems in Paying People Involved in Ministry

- Ministry for most believers is a calling to exercise our gifts, not a paying job. Paul limits people supported for ministry in the church to those, like elders, with major responsibilities (1 Tim 5:17–18), or, like widows, with no other support and serving the Body (1 Tim 5:3–16). Both types of people must meet clear qualifications, and their pay is rightful but not guaranteed (cf. 1 Cor 9:4–18). Even those with a right to support may have to be "tent makers."
- Employees answer to their employer. Therefore do not "employ" those who should answer to someone else. You may temporarily provide scholarships, employ workers, or provide tent-making work for a pastor, but don't employ him as a pastor. A pastor should report to his church, not to foreigners. As soon as possible, ensure that *anyone* who gets outside money reports to a local body that employs them and handles the funds. Their priority needs to be making good decisions for the ministry, not pleasing donors.
- When assistance is given, clarify limitations in time and amount. Open-ended gifts create expectations, often producing frustration and resentment.

Getting On with It

Are these guaranteed methods? Is pursuing sustainability easier? Many years of trial and error testify that sustainability is not the easier goal in the short haul. It involves more involved planning with nationals and difficult decisions. Some "friends" may not stick. *However, we are only servants, and in the end it is their church. It will prosper or fail based on how well they live out their calling from God with the resources God has put in their hands.*

When we think missions, money is one of the first things that comes to our minds. We need to ask God for at least an equal measure of wisdom to use it in ways that will stimulate churches in other countries to stand on their own. If we contribute to their dependence on Western resources we will lose out on another gift—the potential they have to become self-sustaining churches that are our teachers where we are weak. We could learn some lessons from them about ministering in our community, making the Scriptures clear to our culture, learning to be bold and suffer for the name of Christ, and integrating our faith into our own lives and those of the needy people around us. Those who become involved in missions, even for a short-term, often come back with a new perspective, not only on ministry in another culture, but also on ministry in their own.

__Rev. Paul Meiners__ and his wife Liz are long-term missionaries in Africa. Paul's present role is as MTW's Regional Director for Sub Sahara Africa and the Middle East.

Just Who Are the Unreached?

Don Gahagen

Talk about a loaded question! Like many other people, I have battled with and about this question in my missionary career. At the outset, it must be stated that when we say "unreached," we mean "unreached with the gospel of Christ." Many churches have heard the term "unreached," liked its feel and demands, and have dedicated much of their missions giving to "unreached people" somewhere in the world. Things become a bit more difficult when the local missions committee, or mission board for that matter, try to define, characterize, or pinpoint a specific people as being unreached. We even have whole organizations that, through the use of computers, judiciously categorize and track what they consider to be unreached peoples, taking them off the list, as they appear to gain the "reached" status. And if that is not confusing enough, we have the issue of what the Bible means when it talks about "nations" or "peoples."

My intent is not to make an exhaustive, academic, or missiological treatise, but rather to set forth some definitions, principles, and practical applications that may help a missions committee chart its course in this rather difficult landscape.

Defining Unreached and Reached

I am personally involved in a church-planting ministry to the Quechua/Quichua people of the Andes Mountains. As closely as can be determined (a true census is impossible because of the terrain in which they live) there are about twelve million who consider themselves part of this people group. The linguistic experts tell us that there are about forty distinct dialects within the Quechua language. And herein begins the problem of definition.

A video was produced for our ministry that stated that the twelve million Quechua speakers is the largest unreached people group in the Americas. This statement was challenged by one of our own missionaries (from another part of the world) who felt it was an overstatement. Was there not a strong Quechua denomination in the Ayacucho dialect in Peru? Were not whole villages being reported as turning to Christ on the Bolivian Alti Plano? How could we claim unreached status for the Quechua? It was a good and provocative challenge.

Are the followers of Islam an unreached people group? What about the Guatemalan community in Miami; the hundreds of thousands of Chinese speakers in Caracas, Venezuela; the Zulu miners of South Africa; the Polish taxi drivers of Chicago? What needs to be understood is that there are numerous ways to define a people group. It can be done along cultural or linguistic lines, geographic or sociological groupings, or by practical divisions, such as job or function. Almost anything that that creates common affinity for one another can define a people group. Summing up this problem, Dr. Nelson Jennings of Covenant Theological Seminary says, "The multiplicity of peoples making up the diverse human race is what Jesus had in view when he gave His commission to 'disciple the nations.'" The Great Commission's focus is very broad, not compartmentalized. Once a people group is defined, then we move on to whether it is reached or unreached. This definition becomes our next problem.

Any investigation into the subject of unreached people groups will lead us to the giants of missiological thought in this area. Men such as Donald McGavran, Ralph Winter, and Edward Dayton have written extensively on this and related topics, and it is from them that much of what will be said here has come.

Dr. Winter has defined "reached," allowing us to draw our own conclusion on what "unreached" means.

> *A people group can be considered "reached" if there is a body of Christians with the potential to evangelize its own people such that outside, cross-cultural efforts can be "safely" terminated. This potential may be roughly predicted by measuring the percentage of practicing Christians. This figure of 20% has been established by the Lausanne Committee for World Evangelization.* (*Perspectives on the World Christian Movement,* page 316)

So if a people group is 20% Christian, it should be able to reach the remaining 80%, supporting its own ministries. It is further pointed out that this 20% is not a static figure but subject to many variables, such as financial status, education, and location. And there is always the issue of the difference between "Christian" and "evangelical," the latter being of primary concern. Some would go so far as to say that if a group is 2% evangelical, it can be considered reached, but not evangelized.

When we declared the Quechua to be unreached, we calculated that less than 3% were evangelical believers, well below the 20% figure put forth by the Lausanne Committee. We also felt that if we could reach 5% (or better 10%) of a village, it would become a reached village, soon passing the 20% mark. This is because the Quechua tend to live in closed communities where decision-making is communal. Our experience is that if only one family in a village becomes believers, they have a good possibility of bringing others to Christ with only limited outside assistance.

Edward Dayton has pointed out:

> *Another way to explain the difference between reached and unreached is the presence or absence of a viable church. But what do we mean by a viable church? By viable we understand a church that has within itself to spread the good news through the rest of this sociological*

grouping who have a common affinity for one another. (*Perspectives*, page 587)

Putting Definitions into Action

What does all this mean for the local church missions committee wrestling with the desire to be involved in reaching an unreached people group? It means we all need help! Key questions must be asked, such as, "Can our church have its own unreached people group? Are we ready to partner with other churches that have had this same people group laid on their heart by God? How can we find out what people groups are unreached and where they are?" There are several decisions a church has to make before pursuing involvement with a particular people group. First, is there a specific area of the world, religion, or culture to which God is directing our interest? Second, does the church have the desire and ability to commit to this people group over the long haul? A third decision is, to what degree will we be involved (i.e., funding only, personnel only, or funding and personnel)? Most mission work with unreached peoples requires long-term commitment of ten to twenty years. Is the church committing to the unreached group because it is a mission fad or because it feels deeply called to bring this group the gospel?

How much background work has been done before choosing a people group? How accessible is it? Who is already, or soon will be, working with this group? Are we ready to partner with another church or churches, in or out of our denomination or association? What about partnering with other mission agencies, or national organizations to reach this group? Or, do we want to try to "do it ourselves" as some churches have? One church I know planned to pick five unreached people groups, fund the missionary team for that group, adding one new group yearly for five years. It soon became evident that they did not have the expertise or resources to carry out this worthy vision and had to adjust to the reality of the situation. Dr. Sam Larsen of Reformed Theological Seminary gives us another caution: the local church should not rush into redirecting all or most of their mission resources into reaching those classified as unreached to the detriment of other types of mission work.

For several years, I was responsible for helping churches in our denomination with fulfilling their vision for reaching an unreached people group. We were involved with a number of such groups, but helping the church get the information it needed, interacting with missionaries who were working with or close to the group, recruiting and training new missionaries for the task, and maintaining the interest level while all this was taking place was just too much for most churches, and their interest cooled during the process. And sometimes we did not have the information they needed or wanted.

Getting Started

Where does one start this process? Maybe the local church already has picked a group because of their contact with a missionary or mission agency. Perhaps it will be starting from square one with no particular direction in mind. The first place to go would be to MTW to see if the PCA is working with a people group of interest. If not, MTW can connect you with others working with unreached people groups. Get direction from them as how to proceed in becoming involved in their ministry. In reality, while there are many on the list of unreached people groups in the world, many are inaccessible to Western mission agencies and missionaries. A great deal of ingenuity and partnering are required to penetrate these closed or limited-access groups.

Adopt-a-People Clearing House has an extensive listing of unreached people groups, who and where they are, and who is working to reach them. Information such as this can be found at www.mislinks.org.

A Concluding Caution

In conclusion, a word of caution is called for. Damian Efta points out in his article, "Who Are The Unreached" (*Evangelical Missions Quarterly*, January 1994, p. 30) that much good has come from the unreached people movement. It has focused evangelical missions on the Muslim, Hindu, Buddhist, and tribal people of the world. But an unintended consequence has emerged. That consequence is "the arbitrary and extra-biblical division of the world into two groups, reached and unreached, whereas God looks on the world of individuals and sees people as either saved or lost." There is considerable danger when we make reached and unreached the sole criterion for the use of our missionaries and money. Such narrow focus can limit the direction of the Holy Spirit as the Church considers the spiritual needs of the world and its responsibility to meet those needs.

***Rev. Donald Gahagen**, together with his wife Sue, has served as a missionary in Peru, a missions pastor at Coral Ridge PCA, and as MTW's Area Director for Latin America. He continues to work with MTW's Hinterland ministry in South America.*

Short-term Missions: Blessing or Bother?

Dan and Carol Iverson

"*It's not worth the money to send short term missionaries!*" some have said. "Send long-term missionaries or give it to indigenous church planters." Others have said, "Send only those who are fully trained and committed for the long haul."

We hear these concerns. However, as MTW long-term church-planting missionaries working with many two-week and two-year short-term missionaries, we could not be more enthusiastic about their role in kingdom advancement. Sure there is a cost—to the long-term team receiving them, to the ones coming, and to the sending church. But the great benefits to the ministry, to the receiving team, to the sending church, and to the short-term missionary himself far outweigh the cost.

A Great Blessing to the Ministry

From the beginning of our Japan ministry, one- and two-year missionaries have been helping us throw wide the evangelistic net, making hundreds of contacts through our English school, hospitality, concerts, and college ministry. They have also been the workhorses on the field, carrying strategic support roles in finances, and in teaching missionary children. Short-term teams have helped us in broad sowing of the gospel and making new contacts through everything from concerts to English, sports, fun, and friendship. As Mr. Seima Aoyagi, our team's director for the Chiba college ministry, has said:

> *Since Japanese students love to meet and talk to Americans, the short-term missionaries and teams bring us many, many contacts that we Japanese staff could never gather ourselves. They also model a commitment to Christ and His ministry that impacts the new Christian students deeply.*

From Darkness to Light Through Short-term Workers

Mr. Katsuya Shina came to learn English, but instead got the gospel from MTW two-year worker, Dave. Like most Japanese people, Katsuya had never been to church in his life. He says, "I endured the Bible time for several years at the end of each English class, studying it as literature." But God's Word did not return void in Katsuya's life. He testifies now with great thanksgiving of how God used Dave's love, hospitality, and witness to bring him to Christ. Katsuya now leads worship at one church plant. And Dave went on to seminary. He is now the MTW team leader in Thailand.

Follow-up by Email: Hudson Taylor Could Have Never Imagined!

"I am so thankful for Bart and Judy from Orlando," says Mrs. Harumi Soneda, who came to Christ through our team.

> *They came on a two-week mission trip, and did a "home-stay" at our house. I was the only Christian in my family then, but they showed such warmth and love to my husband, my two college daughters, and to me. They invited my daughters to visit them in America the next year. While there, God really opened the eyes of my older daughter, Yoriko, to the gospel through Bart and Judy, and the love they experienced at Orangewood Church.*

Harumi tells with great joy how Yoriko came back to Japan eager to study the Bible. For months, Yoriko emailed her questions about the gospel to Bart and Judy in Florida, and they sent answers bathed in prayer. She joined a Japanese Bible study, began coming to worship, and professed faith some months later. These are Yoriko's words to Bart and Judy:

> *God heard your prayers. Thank you so much. I am very, very thankful . . . My confirmation to live with Him is getting stronger each day. Isn't it great!? He is really working in me. It is so thankful.*
>
> *I know now that He is with me throughout my life (and even more), no matter what happens and no matter what I do . . . I just wanted share this joy with you two. I cannot wait to see you in June!! YORIKO*

By the way, Bart and Judy were reluctant ten-day missionaries, "dragged" to Japan the first time. Half way through the trip, God gave them a heart for missions as they saw the false worship in the Buddhist temples and so many towns with no church of any kind. They now bring a team every year to help share the gospel. They are passionate mobilizers of people, money, and prayer, all because of that first ten-day trip.

Out of the Mouths of Babes—or Sixteen-Year-Olds!

Who would have ever imagined, in this culture where age is so highly venerated, that the life of a sixteen-year-old short-term worker would model the believer's use of the means of grace for a late-forties Japanese believer? Toshiko, the first believer in our team's history, was three years into her new faith when sixteen-year-old Laura came to do a two-week home-stay toward the end of her year in Japan. Toshiko had already observed from a distance the maturity and wisdom of this covenant child. She saw "up close and personal" Laura's daily walk with Christ that included prayer, undivided time in God's Word, and an uncompromising commitment to make worship joyfully central to her week. Toshiko also began to experience the joy and value of appropriating those same means of grace in her own life, and she continues to walk with Christ, mentoring others in the disciplines of grace.

Short-Term Missions Raise Up Career Missionaries

Eighteen-year-old Judith was our first short-term missionary thirteen years ago. Right out of high school, Judith helped home school the kids while Carol met with Japanese ladies. As she also did outreach with Japanese high school girls and helped Dan with team administrative chores, God gave her a heart for Japan. During college she managed the team's prayer mobilization ministry. She returned to Japan after college for two years, stayed for three, and now is back as a proven, able long-term missionary with a passion to reach Japan—and with great language ability since she started young!

Two-week to Two-year to Long-term (and a Sprinkling of Romance)

- **Daniel** came to Japan for a year, came back for two more to teach missionary children and later to help run our team's English outreach ministry to three hundred non-Christian Japanese. He married Mako, one of our first Japanese church members, and recently graduated from seminary.
- **Robert** came for a year at **Daniel's** invitation to teach our team's missionary children, stayed for two years, and now is long-term.
- **Lisa** came for ten days with **Bart and Judy** on their second trip, came back two months later for two years to teach MKs, and is now engaged to **Robert**, preparing to come back together as long-term missionaries.
- **Roberta** came on a short-term trip for ten days, came back for two years, but stayed for three. She ran the team finances as the church-planting budget grew over 25% every year and did evangelism through our English outreach ministry. She is now in her second term as a long-term missionary.
- **Sally** came to Japan for a summer, returned for a year with another mission and now is a second term MTW team member.
- **Craig and Ree** came for a summer, then back for two years, but stayed for three. They are now long-term, serving with Rev. Hirohashi in the Makuhari church plant and as our assistant team leader.
- **Jon** came for a summer, returned for two years of college ministry and now is raising support for long term in order to start our MTW college ministry on another campus.

- **Anne Marie** joined our team for a year at age sixty-six and stayed four years.

There just isn't space to tell all the stories and their impact for the gospel in Japan. Investment in short-term workers is an investment in long-term kingdom work because many return to the field and the others return to their home churches aflame with a mission vision.

Strengthens the Missions Vision of the Sending Church

America may be spiritually needy, but it is one of the most gospel-rich countries on earth. So many who serve short term with our team are gripped by the lostness of Japan and become passionate mobilizers of prayer, finances, and new workers for the harvest.

Short-term Trips Mobilize Prayer

One short-term team came to help with pre-church plant outreach activities in a new Tokyo suburb with no church of any kind. The team was a great help, and we made many new friends and contacts through the special music, English, and outreach events. The team was especially impacted, though, through their participation in our team's monthly four-hour concert of prayer in which we plead with God to pour out His Spirit, ". . . that the desert (of Japan) would become a fertile field, and the fertile field a forest" (Isa. 32:15). We told them about other teams that had gone back to the U.S. with a new vision to pray, and challenged them to do the same. God worked in their hearts. For several years they have gathered monthly to pray for an hour for our team and for Japan. We have seen this over and over again as God uses the two-week or two-year experience to mobilize fervent, informed prayer for kingdom advancement.

Great Spiritual Benefit to the Missionaries' Families

We are eternally grateful for the friendship and blessing that so many short-term missionaries have brought to us. We are especially thankful for the impact on our children.

Raising children on the mission field has been a great blessing. Much of that blessing has come from God via these precious short-term partners in ministry. Often in their late teens or in their twenties, the short-term workers have loved our children and been godly models who were also "cooler" than Dad and Mom. They talked to them of Christ, ministry, and purity. They have given much to our children

The Cost of Short-term Missions

Worker Bees that Take More Work?

The cost of short-term missions is much greater than dollars and cents. The sending church, the short-term missionary, and the receiving team each has time, energy, and effort, expectations and commitments to one another. Our needs encompass the physical, emotional/mental and spiritual "whole people" that we are. It goes without saying, that smooth transition into another culture requires tremendous logistical help, as well as training, ongoing spiritual stimulation, and consistent emotional and mental encouragement. This adjustment period and the more important continuing nurture takes varying amounts of patience, energy, and time on the expatriate members' part. Our experience, overall, has been well worth any investment that's been made! The amount of kingdom fruit may only be known in eternity. But we would be dishonest if we stopped here. There have been cases where the cost to our team has outweighed the benefit of the worker, sadly necessitating their being sent back earlier than expected. There have been times when their needs have far exceeded our capacities, or where we, as a team, have failed to give the necessary time and energy to these brothers and sisters because of ever-increasing ministry demands. Those times have stretched us to develop greater dependence on Christ and they have modeled for the new Japanese believers the power of the gospel in broken lives.

The Ongoing Benefit of Short-term Mission Trips

It has been said that World War II was the greatest short-term missions trip of church history. Thousands of soldiers, sailors, and

Marines returned to the places they had gone on their "short-term trip" armed the second time as long-term workers with the sword of the Spirit. They led a great wave of new mission effort to the end that God be worshiped in every tongue and tribe.

The growing wave today of short-term missions zeal seems certain to have even more impact on the world as tens of thousands of short-termers fan out in missions service around the world. They help move the work forward doing frontline evangelism and discipleship, in support roles behind the scenes, and in teaching missionary children. God often does much *through* them, but even more *to* them through the struggles and blessings they experience. God often uses the experience to call many of them to return long-term in the places where they served short-term. And God sends most back to their homes deeply affected by what they experienced, much more ready in heart and head than most other Christians to mobilize the Church to pray, give and partner with the work on the field.

***Rev. Dan Iverson** and his wife Carol are MTW long-term missionaries who have spent twelve years in Japan. Dan serves as team leader for the Chiba/Tokyo church-planting team.*

Section II—Church Planting: Looking Outward

Why the Church?

Scot Sherman

Eugene Peterson once described the Church as consisting of "equal parts mystery and mess." I agree with him, but it seems that I think about the mess much more than I ever do about the mystery, and I certainly hear more about the mess. I'm constantly meeting people who've left the Church because of some way they've been hurt by the Church or disappointed by Christians. For one reason or another, they left because of the mess.

Being in church leadership doesn't help this problem of perspective. Leaders are relentlessly exposed to the "belly of the beast" at board or agency meetings where dirty laundry is aired and where the list of problems on the docket is longer than the items of praise. Year after year, we watch mission teams fall apart, churches decline, and ministers fall. The cynicism can be hard to fight.

So "why the Church?" That may seem to be a needless or unspiritual question, or at the very least, a cheeky one, but it is a question that many people are asking and therefore, one we need to answer. I have found that when the questions I ask are basic and rudimentary, the answers are often the most illuminating (e.g., Why do I believe there is a God? Why do I believe Jesus is who He said He was?), and I think it is no less the case when it comes to why we think the Church is worth keeping, and certainly for why we think we ought to plant churches all over the world.

As I have wrestled with the realities of "mystery and mess" over the years, the theologian who has been most helpful to me in thinking about the Church has been Lesslie Newbigin, the long-time missionary to South India. His writings and his life's ministry are a clarion call to consider the first principles of the Church's existence. Newbigin was not naïve about the problems of the Church, but he spent his life encouraging Christians to remember that the Church *really is* the mystical body of Christ, the fellowship of the Holy Spirit, the community that has been fully reconciled to God and shares in the divine life of the Trinity.

The Fellowship of New Life

Newbigin encourages us to see the Church, first of all, through the lens of the gospel doctrine of justification by faith. At its most basic level, justification means that through faith in Christ alone we are restored to a right relationship with God, to sharing in his life. An individual who believes the gospel is completely identified and united with Christ in his death and resurrection. But the "actual living context" of this new life is the fellowship of the church. "The new relationship with God in Christ is necessarily also a new relation with all who share it."[1] The gospel not only calls us to renounce independence from God, it also calls on us to renounce independence from others. True spirituality is a spirituality that receives God's grace through the broken vessels of others in the church.

Much so-called spirituality is really an attempt to escape from [God's] method of dealing with us into a mystical and private type of experience which, being purely private, is wholly self-centered.

> *The Gospel does not come to each of us in isolation. It comes to us through a particular book and through a particular fellowship. . . . and that fellowship, like all human fellowships, has maintained its existence in history as a visible organization with visible tests of membership, with officers, rules and ceremonies. It is a false spiri-*

> *tuality, divorced from the teaching of the Bible, which regards this visible and continuing Church as of subordinate importance for the life in Christ. 'Those who have God as Father must have the church as mother.'*[2]

Foretaste of Heaven, Firstfruit of Redemption

Throughout his writings Newbigin refers to the church as a "foretaste of heaven" and a "firstfruit of redemption." The gospel teaches us that the Church is the one and only *foretaste* of heaven now because she alone has a real participation in the life of God on earth. Because the Church shares in this life, she is the *firstfruit* of the reconciliation, restoration, and renewal that will come when Jesus returns, when "the times reach their fulfillment" and God brings "all things in heaven and on earth together under one head, even Christ" (Ephesians 1:10).

This divine reality of foretaste and firstfruit is the key to understanding the Church's power and relevance. The Church is the new community that exists because of Jesus' saving work and the Holy Spirit's eschatological presence. In those churches where His truth and love are evident, there is a genuine experience of salvation here and now. Even if it is only a "foretaste" and incomplete, within the fallen world the Church singularly embodies the restored harmonies about which she bears witness. She not only testifies to reconciliation, she is a living reality of reconciled relationships.

The Church does not merely exist to propagate the message of salvation. She is called to embody its realities:

> *Mission must spring from and lead back into a quality of life which seems intrinsically worth having in itself. If we answer the question "why should I become a Christian?" simply by saying "In order to make other Christians," we are involved in infinite regress. The question "to what end?" cannot simply be postponed to the eschaton . . . the life in Christ is not merely the instrument of the apostolic mission, it is also its end and purpose.*[3]

Newbigin's points ring true even for "the cup is half-empty" cynics like me. For all the disappointments and frustrations I have experienced firsthand with the Church, she has nonetheless been a singular instrument of God's grace in my life. What I know of forgiveness, mercy, and love has been conveyed as a message by the Church, and has also been experienced as a supernatural reality within the life of the Church.

I do not remember a time when I did not believe the gospel, but I do remember the processes of persuasion that led to deeper levels of faith as I grew older. At every step of the way, it was the Church that was the instrument of that deepening commitment. The theological thinkers who influenced me came to me through the fellowship of the Church, as did the friends who encouraged me. The grace that sustained me was through the Word that I heard from the Church and the sacraments I received from the Church. The prayers that protected, shaped, strengthened, and guided me were from within the worship and fellowship of the Church. When I ask myself, "Why has this always been the case?" the answer is simply that the Church is the one and only place where I can know and be in fellowship with Jesus. There may be temptations to leave or criticize the institution, but if the Church is the body of Christ, the sole fellowship of his Spirit, I always come back to the bottom line stated so pointedly by St. Peter: "Lord, to whom shall we go? You have the words of eternal life" (John 6:68). When I stop and consider the matter carefully, the experience of the mystery of the shared life of Jesus in the Church far outweighs and out-"realities" the nagging annoyance of the mess.

The Instrument of Salvation

The Church is our foretaste of heaven and a credible sign before a watching world of the salvation of our God. It is imperative that we understand the Church's calling to be *the* instrument of bringing the message of salvation to the world. Newbigin was passionate and wrote extensively in the last years of his life about this "missional" calling of the Church. He cautioned against mission as a utilitarian rationale for the Church, i.e., thinking that "the Church exists only to proclaim the gospel." He argued that it is precisely because the Church is not merely instrumental, but a present foretaste of heaven and sign of redeemed life and restored relationships that she can be instrumental.

How important is it for the Church to be engaged in mission (evangelism, church planting, etc)? For Newbigin, it is of the Church's very essence as a sharer of the life of Christ. The mission to seek and save the lost is, after all, Christ's mission! Newbigin quotes Emil Brunner's famous quip, "the Church exists by mission as fire exists by burning," then continues:

> *It is impossible to reconcile with the New Testament the view, which seems to be more or less accepted among the majority of [church leaders], that while missionary work is an admirable thing to do, within reasonable limits, it is not something without which the church simply falls to the ground. We must say bluntly that when the Church ceases to be a mission, then she ceases to have any right to the titles by which she is adorned by the New Testament. Apart from actual engagement in the task of being Christ's ambassador to the world, the name "priests and kings unto God" is but a usurped title.*[4]

Newbigin gives equal ultimacy to the callings of the Church to be body of Christ and the mission of Christ, of being a Spirit-filled fellowship and a Spirit-empowered instrument of salvation. Much of the present discouragement about the Church is a result of the experience of imbalance in either or both of these callings. Those over-zealous for one calling over the other should listen carefully to Newbigin's nuanced description of the "ecosystem" of salvation. The only hermeneutic of the gospel is the congregation that lives out the gospel. A church truly effective in mission is a church that demonstrates in her own life and relationships the transcendent life of God.

> *Just as we insist that a Church which has ceased to be a mission has lost the essential character of a Church, so must also say that a mission which is not at the same time truly a Church is not a true expression of the divine apostolate. An unchurchly mission is as much a monstrosity as a unmissionary Church.*[5]

What Do We "Do" About the Church?

Reformed Christians believe that before God we are "at the same time, righteous and sinners." The same also holds true for the Church corporately. She is holy in Christ and sinful because of us. To despair for the Church is nothing less than to despair for ourselves and our salvation. Even worse, it is to despair for Christ and for His promises to build His Church. His commitment to me is His commitment to His Church.

If we believe the gospel, we must believe in the Church. Because we believe the gospel, we have renewed hope for the reform and renewal of the Church. It really is, after all, the foretaste, firstfruit, and instrument of the salvation of the Lord. So, what do we need to "do" about the Church? I think Newbigin sets us on the right course: *we need to recommit ourselves to mission* and *we need to recommit ourselves to one another*.

The latter recommitment may be the more challenging, frankly. The greatest cynicism about the Church is not within the Church but outside her walls. Aside from general perceptions of judgmentalism and smug self-righteousness, the world perceives the hollowness of our claims to be "one." We bear a message of reconciliation to the world, but in our own relationships we Protestants alone have produced 35,000 visibly separated denominations (and counting). Newbigin likened multi-divided churches proclaiming reconciliation to temperance societies whose members are perpetually drunk! It is scandalous.

When I was church planting in Greenwich Village, in conversation after conversation with non-Christians, I encountered lists of reasons why they rejected or struggled with Christianity. At or near the top of most of those lists was the scandal of divided Christians. At first, I defended us with Bible verses about truth and detailed discussions of Church history. That never worked, even once. At some point during that time I began reading Newbigin, and rereading my New Testament in light of what he was saying. Instead of defending, I started repenting and admitting to my non-Christian friends that they were right about us. This is scandalous and we are hypocritical. But I pointed out that it was the gospel that enables Christians to face the failure of our love for one another. When my love fails, there is still a love that never fails. People began to listen and were attracted (and surprised) by the humility. Apologetics by apology!

I began to realize something then about the mess: it never helps to deny that it is there, or make excuses for it. But when we humble ourselves and acknowledge our failure, we come back to our most fundamental calling as the Church: to confess that we are sinners in need of the Savior, which is the mystery the world longs to see revealed.

***Rev. Scot Sherman** is the senior pastor of Intown Community Church (PCA) in Atlanta, GA. He was the organizing pastor of The Village Church in Greenwich Village, in New York City.*

1. Lesslie Newbigin, *The Reunion of the Church* (London: SCM Press, 1948), p. 97. For an extended discussion of the implications of the doctrine of justification, see pp. 84–103.
2. *The Reunion of the Church*, p. 29. The last sentence is a quote from Calvin's *Institutes* (IV:1:1), in which Calvin quotes St. Cyprian.
3. Lesslie Newbigin, *The Household of God* (London: SCM Press, 1953), p. 147.
4. *The Household of God*, p. 141.
5. *The Household of God*, p. 148.

Toward a Definition of Church-Planting Movements

Paul D. Kooistra

There has been much written and discussed in recent years about church-planting movements. There is also significant debate about just what it is. It has proven an elusive subject to describe with precision or finality.

What follows is not intended to be definitive, but rather is an attempt to move us toward a more complete and accurate understanding regarding the key characteristics of a church-planting movement. I hope that it deepens our understanding and agreement, and as a result spurs us to further dialogue and action.

A Definition

A church-planting movement (CPM) is a God-glorifying, God-centered work of His grace whereby the Holy Spirit energizes indigenous leaders to plant a cluster of churches with a common vision and purpose to reproduce themselves often by means of evangelizing and discipling a specific region or people group.

Such movements balance orthodoxy, unity, and liberty, and are built upon indigenous structures and institutions, as well as local funding and especially native worship.

The focus of these movements is the transformation of all of life by encouraging the fulfillment of a culture's highest good through the Lordship of Jesus Christ.

Commentary

Church-Planting Movement: Donald McGavran coined the concept of "people movements" to Christ in his landmark book *The Bridges of God* first published in the United Kingdom in 1955.[1] Basic to his argument was the opinion that Western Christianity, because of its dominant individualistic world and life view, is blinded to how most people come to Christ. Historically, the vast majority of converts have come in groups, tribes, villages, ethnic groups, as a single unit. Chuo Wee Hiar writes, the Western self-conscious states, "I think, therefore I am." For most of the rest of the world it is, "I participate, therefore I am."[2]

People Movements: Don McGavran argued that people movements have five considerable advantages. First, they create permanent churches in many places through the movement of God's Spirit. Second, they are naturally indigenous. Third, they are a spontaneous and natural expansion of the Church. Fourth, they have enormous possibility for growth. The fifth advantage is that these movements provide a sound pattern of becoming a Christian. People and their environments change through the gospel from the inside out.

God-glorifying/God-centered: A CPM cannot be built on the foundation of missiology, church-planting methodology, cultural anthropology or any other important discipline. As William Ortega writes, ". . . a church-planting movement is not an end in itself. The end of all of our efforts is for God to be glorified."[3] I would further argue that any kingdom work that is not totally dependent on God with a single purpose of magnifying Christ will, in the end, be found hollow and with little enduring existence.

Holy Spirit: Gary Waldecker has written a very excellent book entitled, *Toward a Theology of Movements: Missiology from a Kingdom Perspective*. This is a fine work, which I believe could be widely useful. He develops a theology of movements around seven subordinate movements. The third, the outward movement, is a work of God's Spirit whereby we drink of Christ and one small sip produces whole rivers, which flow out of us to bless those around us. Gary states,

> *The task before us is not difficult—it is impossible. However, the Lord will do the impossible through us. As the Lord commanded the man with the withered hand to stretch it out, as He commanded the paralytic to stand and walk, and as He commanded Peter to walk to Him on the water, so we must attempt the impossible, trusting only in the supernatural power of Christ, refusing dependence on "safer" methods. This is the work that can only be accomplished in the power of the Holy Spirit.*[4]

Indigenous: One of the most important, if not the most important element of a CPM, is that it is mainly indigenous. For a church to impact a culture it must be of that culture. This seems from the beginning to be built into God's design for His body on earth—the Church. Modern students of New Testament manuscripts first thought that the Greek, which was much corrupted from Classical Greek, was the consequence of human errors caused by many years of copying error. Not until Egyptian papyrus manuscripts were studied, did scholars realize that New Testament Greek was simply the common market place language of the day. In other words, God's holy and inspired Word was written in the common "indigenous" Greek of the marketplace. A church-planting movement must be no less indigenous. First, in the development of leadership, God does not work outside of people, and He always raises up leaders within any people with whom He is working. It is for this reason that a biblical pattern for ministerial training is best served when it is an integral part of real ministry. To take men out of a certain sub-culture and train them in an academic seminary so removes them from the people they came from that they often cannot reach these same people when they return. Secondly, the church must have indigenous direction. A culture is transformed by those who understand, love, and can critique that culture. Culture is so much a part of who we are and what we think that, like language, those who develop within its bounds will better understand its nuances. Finally, for a church to last, it must be indigenously supported. History is full of examples of unhelpful dependence. This does not mean that there is not a place for outside financial assistance. Chapters eight and nine of II Corinthians are all about the churches of Macedonia giving to help the church in Jerusalem. But outside giving must be strategic giving and cannot replace or supercede indigenous giving. If it does, then when that funding no longer exists, the structures of the church will also cease.

A cluster of churches within a specific people or region with a common vision: Some have criticized any emphasis such as this as unbiblical. It is no doubt true, that to be the body of Christ, an exclusionary goal for a church cannot be tolerated. If, on the other hand, the singleness of focus is for outreach to a people that need evangelization and discipling, then it makes a lot of sense. Things usually don't happen until someone gives his or her full attention to the matter. In the same manner, a people are usually not reached until someone says "This is my passion. I will give my life to reach these people."

Reproducing: George Patterson, who has specialized in church multiplication, teaches that healthy churches are "born to reproduce."[5] Such churches emphasize obedience to Christ and the training of leaders who believe that ministry is always reaching out. The Spirit-led church focuses on those outside, not inside, the church. It is not an accident that the Great Commission is the last words of Christ to His Church. This is the purpose of the Church. To rivet the energy of the Church inward can only lead to spiritual constipation.

Balance: A church must be structured exclusively according to God's Word. The church belongs to Him, and He alone has the authority to call it into existence and to shape it for the purpose of reflecting His holy character. When churches add either the best notions or desires of men to biblical orthodoxy, they soon reflect the earthly culture they are a part of and little of the heavenly ethos for which they were created. At the same time, orthodoxy must not kill biblical unity and love. Christ says that a new law or command will rule His kingdom: "Love one another as I have loved you" (John 13:34–35). Doctrine and unity cannot trump one another. They must serve one another, and a church with no love is no more a biblical church than is a church that ignores scriptural teaching to embrace the philosophies of men. Finally, a church must possess liberty. Church-planting movements have always had elements of surprise in them. As we have already stated, we cannot dictate to the Holy Spirit how He will proceed. Worship, fellowship, and structures must reflect the scripture, but in the eternal wisdom of the Holy Spirit they will also reflect the culture. God, whose nature cannot be fully measured, is also the God of variety.

Fulfillment of a culture: Here the choice of words reflects the debate over how culture and faith intersect and even overlap. This is never an easy question. In the Jerusalem Council, Paul uses the argument, in opposition to the Judaizers, that not even Titus, who was with Paul, was compelled by the apostles to be circumcised (Galatians 2:3). Paul claims Titus has become a living example that the gospel and the culture were in conflict. Nevertheless, earlier in Paul's ministry, he had Timothy, his other son in Christ, circumsized in order to enhance the gospel within the culture (Acts 16:3). When does one take a prophetic posture challenging the culture for the sake of the gospel, and when does one accommodate the culture for the sake of the gospel? Obviously, this is not always an easy decision, and one needs all the wisdom of God's Word and the guidance of His Holy Spirit. We must acknowledge that the question of culture is a very sensitive issue today within the world of missions. In the past I have used the phrase, "change culture," but this suggests a lack of appreciation for a culture in which the gospel is preached. Such an emphasis can also have the effect of making the gospel look foreign and hostile to the customs and history of an indigenous people. Phrases such as "penetrate" or "impact" have seemed to me to be more acceptable, but they also contain a somewhat "in your face" connotation as one considers the dynamics of faith and culture. The phrase, the fulfillment of a culture, may help us to get closer to a biblical perspective on this issue. Obviously if the gospel is God's redeeming work within His fallen creation, then all of life, including culture, must be somehow altered by this mighty act of God. I am suggesting that when God calls His creation back to Himself, He intends not to destroy that creation, but to restore it to its original glory. Therefore, when the gospel affects a culture, that culture is moved toward all that it was intended to be. Life is elevated, liberty is heartened, government serves, integrity is valued; even the environment is more universally enjoyed and protected. Human cultures, all of them, were affected by the fall. The gospel reverses that decay.

***Dr. Paul Kooistra** served as president of Covenant Theological Seminary from 1983–1994, and since that time has served the PCA as Coordinator of Mission to the World.*

1. Donald McGravran, *The Bridges of God,* World Dominnion Press, 1955
2. Chuo Wee Hair, "Evangelization of Whole Families," *Perspectives on the World Christian Movement,* Edited by Ralph D. Winter and Steven G. Hawthorrne, 1999, p. 615
3. byhisgrace.com/wortega/CPM.htm,William Ortega
4. Gary Waldecker, *Toward a Theology of Movements: Missiology from a Kingdom Perspective* (summary version), p. 14
5. George Patterson, "The Spontaneous Multiplication of Churches," *Perspectives on the World Christian Movement,* Edited by Ralph D. Winter and Steven Hawthorne, p. 604

Under the Mango Tree: Church Planting Movement in the Philippines

Paul Taylor

"All important decisions are made under the mango tree." So goes the old Filipino saying. On a Sunday afternoon in May of 1993, three missionaries, six Filipino men, and one Filipino woman met under a mango tree to study the Bible. This tree was in Kuya Benji's yard in the peaceful country village of Talang. Floating like an island in a sea of bright green rice fields, under the watchful eye of Mount Arayat, Talang embodies all that is typical of the Filipino country village—strong family relationships, peaceful rural setting, hard working people and strong religious (albeit misled) convictions.

This Bible study under the mango tree was the first gathering in the initial church planting work of MTW-Philippines. Kuya Rap sat next to me with his huge Catholic Bible opened in his lap, continually interrupting with good questions that helped all to think more deeply about the gospel message that was being told. Rap, Benji and the others present invited friends for the next week. By the third week about twenty were gathered, and following the invitation that day, six made commitments to follow Christ. These were the first believers in what was to become Talang Bible Christian Church. That church became the first of many in what we trust will eventually become a strong Reformed and covenantal church-planting movement. It all began under the mango tree.

In the nine years since those first meetings under Benji's mango tree, over fifty church-planting projects have begun. Almost all of the churches have survived and become part of the Presbyterian Church of the Philippines.

A Vision Is Born

On a Sunday in 1990, Sarah and I were quietly sitting in worship at Parkview PCA in Lilburn, Georgia, when the Lord spoke to each of us separately, urging us to commit to foreign missions. At that time, Sarah was enjoying life serving on the staff of Intown Community Church (PCA), and I was serving as Coordinator of Church Planting for Mission to North America. We were both very content in our work, and would have enjoyed staying there forever. After the service, however, we compared notes and concluded that indeed the Lord was calling to us pursue opportunities overseas. So we began discussions with MTW leadership about our future.

As we were meeting with MTW Coordinator, John Kyle, one day, he suggested that Manila, Philippines, might be a good spot for us. Soon we found ourselves in a plane that was landing in Manila for a two-week exploratory trip that was to change the course of our entire future ministry. During those two weeks Filipino church leaders and mission leaders unanimously expressed that the greatest need was not more schools, not more evangelistic meetings, but more churches. Given our twenty-three years experience in church planting, we felt confirmed in our decision to move to Manila.

June 1992 was the month we arrived. Immediately we started fifteen months of language and cultural acquisition. It was eleven months into that study that the mango tree Bible study was held, resulting in the first church. During language study we also committed to working with Pastor Bob Enoya to develop churches around Taal Lake, two hours south of Manila. And Pastor Dado Fonacier asked us to be his consultant in a new church-planting work on the campus of the University of the Philippines in Los Baños.

But all of these works—Talang, Taal and Los Baños were in rural or small town settings, and we knew that our main focus should be on Manila's twelve million people—now estimated at 13.6 million. So in January of 1994, we moved into the city, knowing it was God's plan, but not knowing the strategy.

A Vision for the City

Pastor Dado asked me to come preach at Los Baños on Sunday February 6, 1994. Arriving there the night before, I stayed with a member family overnight. In the morning, while having devotions and preparing to speak, the strategy for the future suddenly became clear. It was almost as if the Lord had spoken out loud:

- Thrust to the City—starting twenty-five churches in Metro Manila, with each starting a daughter church within four years from its first public worship service.
- Thrust to the Province—starting twenty-five churches in the provincial areas with each starting a daughter church within four years from its first public worship service.
- Thrust to the World—sending out twenty Filipino missionaries to cross-cultural or overseas places of service before the work became ten years old.

As I shared this with the team at the next team meeting, this strategy was adopted.

During our language study time we had spent much time networking with Filipino church leaders and mission leaders. And since some Korean missionaries were forming the Presbyterian Church of the Philippines, we built bridges to and developed relationships with the leaders of this young denomination. In addition, we had asked four key Filipino leaders to be an advisory board for us. As we made our strategy known, those leaders we had gotten to know referred some potential Filipino church-planting pastors to us.

To guide us in our recruiting, we had developed several key commitments:

- We would start Reformed and covenantal churches and thus, needed pastors with those commitments.

- Every new church would be started with a Filipino senior pastor from day one.
- The target audience was the professional and business community of Manila.
- We would seek the best church-planting pastors possible.
- In order for us to recruit the best pastors, for them to be free of care and able to focus on their work, they would be well supported.
- Our financial support would be short-term, reducing each year, and for three years only.
- We would develop careful and intensive training and supervision.
- Each church planter must pass some level of presbytery exams before becoming an approved church planter.

Those early days were heady and exciting ones. February 22, 1994 was the first of the monthly pastors' fellowship meetings that have continued until this day. These monthly meetings have become the heart of the work—times of fellowship, prayer, instruction, building "esprit de corps," and planning.

A Commitment to Evangelism

The first two urban church-planting pastors were placed and began their work in April. We had learned through networking that developing Evangelistic Bible Studies (EBS) was the most effective means of finding people to start a new church. The church planter would find people for the studies through referral or his own door-to-door work.

Pastor Edwin Roxas was the first of the urban church planters. Edwin made a commitment to himself and the Lord that he would spend three hours each day out on the streets "finding people." After the first day he called me and said, "This is such hard work!" To encourage him, I spent the next few days doing it with him. As he discovered that he was more effective than I was, his commitment was strengthened. Within two weeks he had twelve Evangelistic Bible Studies that he led each week. This became typical of the future church planters as well.

Our plan was for each EBS to run for about ten to twelve weeks, after which the converts were put into what we called a "Foundational Bible Study." The initial EBS was discontinued and the process would begin again with more door-to-door work and referral resulting in new Evangelistic Bible Studies. The Foundational Bible Study was given that name because it was the foundation for the new church which would begin to hold worship in due time.

As time went by, we discovered that most who made genuine professions of faith (people whose lives were obviously changed) never found their way into our churches. That told us that if we wanted one hundred members in a new church, approximately four to five hundred would have to come to Christ before those one hundred would be found in our church. Consistent, persistent, ongoing, never-ending evangelism become the byword of the church planting work.

Constant encouragement and close supervision were crucial to the effectiveness of the work. We found with experience that each missionary supervisor could only adequately oversee four or five works. In our weekly time with each church-planting pastor we would spend three or four hours doing what was most needed in that project—making new contacts, meeting with developing leaders in the church, consultation with the pastor, etc.

Typically it would take twelve months of this sort of work for each new congregation to be ready for its first public worship service. These first public services became great milestones for each church.

A Hallmark of Training

In addition to extensive evangelism, intensive training soon became a hallmark of the work. Some was formal training. Pastors who came to us from outside the Presbyterian Church of the Philippines were required to take twenty-four units of study at Presbyterian Theological Seminary. And those few who hadn't yet completed at least a Bachelor of Theology degree were required to do so.

Some training was informal. This took the form of church-planting seminars at the beginning and after each six months of a pastor's service. Informal training also took place through instruction at the monthly pastors' fellowship and occasional special seminars. And lots of one-on-one training occurred in interviews with potential church planters and in weekly consultative meetings.

Three ministries have been emphasized since they are crucial to the Filipino context:

- **Mercy**: About 50% of Filipinos live in poverty and have great medical, nutritional and other basic needs. We have come to realize that, in a country where poverty abounds, mercy ministry must also abound in the church. A church that is not involved in mercy ministry is marginalized, viewed as a church concerned only for itself—a church without a heart. So churches have been encouraged to develop nutritional ministries, ministry to street children and medical ministries, all accompanied, of course, with biblical instruction and evangelism. All of these mercy activities are expanding into effective programs with many churches involved in each.
- **Missions**: Filipinos are very adaptable people, easily learn languages, can live frugally, and understand Asian, Latin and Western culture. They make great missionaries. This sending aspect will be a great part of the future of the work.
- **Multiplication**: Bob Logan, the church growth guru, tells us that, if a church hasn't planted its first daughter church within three years, it probably never will. We have amended that standard a bit, encouraging the new churches to start a daughter church within four years of its first public worship service. Of the first fifty churches, thirty-six were mother churches, eleven were daughter churches, and three were granddaughter churches.

A Look Ahead

After the initial four years of work, more and more Filipinos were placed in leadership. Five church-planting pastors were given the role of supervisor, so that these men are now doing most of the supervision. Many have become moderators, chairmen and members of General Assembly and presbytery committees.

What will the future hold? Will this work really become a Reformed and covenantal church-planting movement fully led and moved along by Filipino leadership? Will a great number of new Filipino Christians be mobilized for world missions? Will the Presbyterian Church in the Philippines become a dynamic denomination, molding the thinking of Filipino society? But above all will the Lord's name be honored and glorified in the minds and hearts of more and more Filipino people? This is our prayer—that the church may grow out from under the mango tree, and on to the ends of the earth for the honor and glory of our King.

Rev. Paul Taylor *is MTW's International Director for Asia. He was formerly Church Planting Director for Mission to North America, and he and his wife, Sarah, have been missionaries to the Philippines for ten years.*

Lateral Leadership: The Case for Facilitation as an Emerging Church-Planting Model

BILL RIBOCHAUK

When I think of church-planting facilitation, several pictures come to mind. They are mental pictures of three potential church-planting movement leaders who have blessed me with their friendship. One is Western European; the other two are Middle Eastern. They are men whom I want to facilitate. And I'm not sure I know how.

While there are many facets of church-planting-movement leadership, there is one over-all criterion that is, without a doubt, critical to movement leadership: vision. Roger Fisher, in a book on managing conflict, tells of a story in Italian folklore about three stonecutters.[1] When asked what they were doing, the first replied, "Cutting these stones to the exact size necessary." The second replied, "Earning my wages." The third replied, "Building a cathedral."

If by facilitation we mean empowerment, then I would suggest that stonecutters number one and number two are not ready for facilitation. Thomas Graham, in a paper on empowering leadership,[2] proposes that models of leadership need to be matched to the competency and commitment level of those being led. He suggests that people lacking competency and commitment should be led using direct supervisory models. Only those with high competency and commitment levels should be led with empowering models of supervision.

The whole idea of supervision, however, seems antithetical to facilitation. Or is it? Might we more appropriately ask, "Can we lead when we are not in charge?" A critical aspect of directing others is job knowledge. Knowing what people are supposed to do, make, produce, etc. and the methods required are crucial to management. That kind of management is essential in direct supervisory models.

However, because of the dynamics of social interaction in cross-cultural situations, it is hard to adapt patterns of thought and behavior (even simple tourist-like thought and behavior) to new cultures. The necessary translation is more than just learning a new vocabulary. Even direct supervisory management becomes difficult in these situations. For example, while studying at the Goethe Institute in Atlanta, we had a teacher who worked in marketing for Mercedes-Benz, USA. He said that German managers would get extremely frustrated when they incorrectly used the English false cognate "may" for the German word "mag." What they wanted to imply was compulsory action rather than voluntary action; instead American employees heard that they had permission to do or not to do a specific thing. In such cases, how can empowering facilitation be effective?

Several years ago I heard PCA pastor, Mark Gornik, speak about his work in Sandtown, an inner city, African-American neighborhood in Baltimore, Maryland. His approach to entering that community in the posture of a learner, followed by loving service based on what he had learned, allowed him to eventually lead from a "lateral" or "side-by-side," rather than a "top-down" position.

In a book entitled, *Getting It Done: How to Lead When You're Not in Charge*, by Roger Fisher and Alan Sharp, the authors outline problems encountered when leaders "talk down" to their followers.[3] They have observed, "Telling others what to do implies that they have lower status. All of us are concerned with ourselves. Whatever you say, your words will be heard in terms of what they imply about the listener, and the relationship between you."[4] This is especially true in cross-cultural relationships.

North Americans are often viewed by people in host cultures as talking down to others. Whether the accusation is just or not is beside the point if you are the one who is trying to get your ideas across. In a facilitative approach to leadership, great discipline and commitment are required to keep others in positions of superiority where they are willing to accept ideas and suggestions.

One-Anothering

A model of relationship building that our teams have begun to use in our facilitation of national pastors in Europe and Asia follows the principles of the "one-another commands" of Scripture. We put a great deal of emphasis on the first level: greet one another well. We base this first level on the scriptural injunction to "greet one another with a holy kiss."

When we lived in a small village in the Middle East, our boys used to meet an older man coming up our street every day from the mosque. They would be going out of the house just about the time that Mr. Abdul was coming by. The boys would take his proffered hand in theirs, raise the back of it to their mouths, and give it a kiss. Then they would place the clasped hands—his and theirs—to their foreheads, hold them still for a minute and then place them finally over their hearts before letting go.

In essence they were taking this gentleman's greeting, making it holy with their kiss and then placing his greeting in their minds and hearts. They were signifying that they were ready to sit at his feet and learn from him. If we are going to facilitate national pastors and church-planting movement leaders we can do no less. Our attitude needs to be one of humble learning.

The second level of the one-another commands that we emphasize is serving one another well. By greeting well we earn the right to serve well. In fact, our service is apt because it has been informed by our greeting process.

In serving well, we will be invited by those whom we serve to enter the third level of the one-another relationship—loving well.

Mark Gornik points out that the service that he and his wife had given to the residents in Sandtown was based on information they had gleaned over months and months of listening. They listened to the oral histories of the families in the neighborhood. It was no surprise then that their African-American neighbors expressed how loved they felt by the Gornik's service.

It is only after loving well that we ever earn the right to enter the fourth level of one-another relationship—exhorting one another well. Perhaps because we value directness in our culture, Americans are perceived in an unjust light. But we do like to exhort others, don't we? It comes so naturally. Right away. Often before we have greeted or served or loved the recipient of our exhortations.

Learning Together

Facilitation is easier to talk about than to practice. As a relatively new ministry region in Mission to the World, we are still learning the hard way—the school of experience. In 1996 our stated purpose was to:

1) Identify, recruit, train, and facilitate Reformed and covenantal national church-planting movement leaders and national church-planting pastors.
2) Identify, recruit, train, and deploy teams of expatriate facilitators to work with the national movement leaders and national pastors.
3) Assemble networks of international Reformed & covenantal churches to support and assist in this process.

We are presently working with a number of potential church-planting movement leaders. We have learned much from each of them. Early in 2003 the men we have identified as potential church-planting movement leaders will meet to help us identify what it is that makes them who they are. Mission to the World's Global Training and Development Team has already produced an initial study on what it means to be a church-planting facilitator. The potential movement leaders will also interact with us on how well we have defined that process.

Since 1997 we have also deployed a host of expatriate teams. Each year we have conducted training in Muslim immigrant enclaves in Europe, preparing new team members for facilitative church planting. We have developed an approach that encompasses five areas of proficiency[5]:

1) evangelism/discipleship
2) preaching/teaching the Word
3) church-planting facilitation
4) cross-cultural adaptation
5) high-performance teaming

In many ways these areas overlap, like Olympic rings. In some areas, like cross-cultural adaptation and high-performance teaming, the circle might envelop almost all we do in other areas.

As we continue to listen carefully to those we serve about their backgrounds, contexts, hopes and dreams, we are developing new and better ways to serve. We are adding new competencies to our list of work practices. We are more committed than ever to facilitative leadership. Lately we think we are really starting to love our church-planting partners and they are starting to love us.

In terms of our third goal, the establishment of support and assistance networks, we are just beginning. We have had a number of PCA churches work with us as we have deployed teams. An exchange of short-term workers and visitors has occurred in both directions. We have formed partnerships to formalize relationships between the churches serving and the churches being served. Facilitative leadership at this level is the most important.

We hope that in the final analysis, a level of interdependence between churches planted and churches planting will occur. We hope that the level of empowerment, the spirit of cooperation and the love that grows out of mutual service will be so compelling to those around, that the Church will multiply in the areas of both the host and guest churches at an increasing rate.

The Way of the Cross

Joseph E. Stiglitz, a Nobel Prize winner for his work in analyzing the imperfections of financial markets, has recently written a book entitled *Globalization And Its Discontents*.[6] In it he compares the heavy-handedness of the International Monetary Fund in relation to emerging Two-Thirds World economies, with domino-theory politics of the '50s and '60s. Essentially he says, "The big guy is making the little guy comply to quick-fix remedies that the big guy has dreamed up."

This analysis is over-simplistic in both cases—financially and militarily. I think we can learn something in terms of missiology, however, from his analysis. We could cite many historical cases where do-gooders have gone into totally unfamiliar areas, thinking that they knew exactly how to make things better—financially, socially, politically, etc.—and with disastrous results.

This is not the way of the cross. Our calling is to a more complicated, yet loving service. Lateral leadership. Empowerment. Real partnership. Facilitation. And perhaps we help the most, when we recognize that we "don't know how."

__Mr. Bill Ribochauk__ is a consultant for MTW's work in Europe and Asia.

1. Roger Fisher, *Beyond Machiavelli: Tools For Coping With Conflict*, Penguin Books, New York, N.Y., 1994, p. 67
2. Thomas Graham, "Empowering Leadership," Center for Organizational & Ministry Development, 1995
3. Roger Fisher & Alan Sharp, *Getting It Done: How to Lead When You're Not in Charge*, Harper Collins, New York, N.Y., 1995, p. 16
4. ibid.
5. The first three areas of proficiency were suggested to me by Steve Childers in a conversation about church-planting movements
6. Joseph E. Stiglitz, *Globalization And Its Discontents*, W.W. Norton & Company, New York, N.Y. 2000

Section III—Partnership: Looking Together

From Patron to Partner

Scott Seaton

The Untraditional Becomes Tradition

Shortly after the publication of his *Enquiry Into the Obligation of Christians*, in 1792, William Carey addressed ministers of the Baptist Association at a meeting in Nottingham, England. After encouraging them from Isaiah 54:2–3 to commit themselves to world evangelization, he exhorted them to demonstrate faith: "Expect great things from God; attempt great things for God." The next day, at great financial sacrifice to themselves, they formed a missions board, the Baptist Missionary Society. With this commitment, the modern missions movement was born. While the current of missions runs all the way back to Eden, so influential were Carey's writings, model, and methods that a truly new channel had been opened.

Much has changed downstream since Carey's day. The increased emphasis on indigenous leadership, the evolving role of the missionary, and the concept of unreached people groups are some of the many ways missions has matured in the last two hundred years. Yet the basic method for sending and supporting missionaries remains largely untouched. Simply stated, churches that share a passion for missions would entrust their members and resources to a mission agency, which would oversee all aspects of field ministry.

The Baptist Missionary Society served not only as the means to support these early missionaries to India, it became a model for all subsequent efforts. It remains the dominant model today.

This approach tends to be very linear and one-directional, with the church laying the foundation for missions in education, prayer, and support, but then essentially turning over all further responsibility to the sending agency. In turn, the agency would—hopefully—provide a well-developed system of oversight and support, a breadth of ministry opportunities and experience, a coherent philosophy of ministry, and a mechanism to pool resources. As a model, it was straightforward, uncomplicated, and directly responsible for the expansion of world missions to this day.

The following diagram portrays that relationship:

Traditional Model

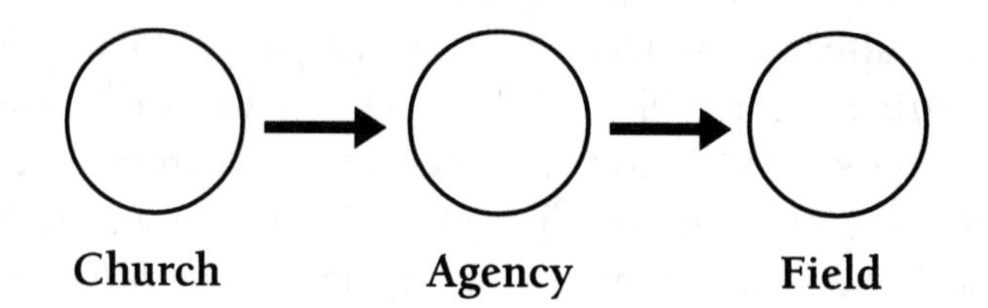

Agency: "Here's what we're doing. Come be a part of it."

For all that was gained in this approach, two significant weaknesses emerged. First, the local church largely delegated its ownership of missions to the agency—and along with it a significant amount of passion and vision for the work in the field. The local church was rarely involved in field ministry, except through praying for the work and hearing from the missionaries. The actual ministry became the province of the agency. The downside of this approach is that the local church was effectively relegated to the role of patron, rarely questioning what ownership of actual missions work it should have. Both the church and the agency accepted this relationship as unassailable.

Second, this passivity inevitably leads to churches having little direction for their missions ministry—a purposelessness rarely shared by other ministries of the church. The church rightfully expects its children's ministry to have a philosophy and structure. Same for adult education or worship. But in many churches, the missions ministry has no such focus. The primary role of the missions committee is sadly reduced to that of a foundation distributing grant money to applicants. It's simply assumed that this is all that missions committees do. No wonder there's not much passion for world missions in many of our churches.

As a missions pastor for fourteen years, I would often receive calls from both missionaries and agencies, seeking our support for their ministry. The conversation usually went something like this: "Here's what we're doing in missions. God is opening a strategic door for ministry, and we'd like you to be part of it—by giving us your money and your people." I often felt like I was being sold something, with no concern whether we had a prior interest in the "product." Until we began to be intentional about our involvement, we would passively receive many such requests, making decisions on little more than the quality of the presentation and the availability of funds. We were not much more than patrons.

A Demand for More Ownership

Today, however, people expect more involvement. Younger generations are less willing to entrust others with their resources and loyalty, instead demanding hands-on experience and ownership. Further, in a day of rapid travel and instant communication, church missions leaders and members are now able to participate directly in cross-cultural missions with little inconvenience or sacrifice. Short-term projects and instant connection to the field via email are common examples of this trend. When coupled with greater resources to sustain that interest, it's no surprise that the traditional model is being rejected in many churches.

Rather than passively responding to a variety of requests and strategies, these churches are thoughtfully developing a missions emphasis that uniquely suits their congregation. Based on their philosophical commitments and personal relationships, for example, a church may want to focus on church planting among a certain people group. Such a focus invariably means concentrating on a few places in order to have greater impact and involvement. Depth rather than breadth becomes the overriding consideration. This commitment often involves taking the initiative in helping to develop the ministry, and thus more ownership in its success or failure. In this way, churches begin to assume more of the responsibilities traditionally reserved for the sending agency. From the recruitment of missionaries to the development of strategy, some churches are becoming, in theory and sometimes in practice, their own mission agencies.

This approach is one of the most significant trends in missions today, and some churches in the PCA have taken steps in this direction. Some of this momentum stems from the churches' perception of sending agencies as bureaucratic and staid, unable or unwilling to involve the local church and its missions' priorities—even unaware it might have any. In that climate, the church feels it has no choice but to go it alone. The dominant message in this model is the church saying, in effect, "We don't want to delegate all the exciting stuff to an agency. We can do it ourselves."

The following diagram portrays that relationship, where the missions agency is bypassed altogether:

Church as Sending Agency

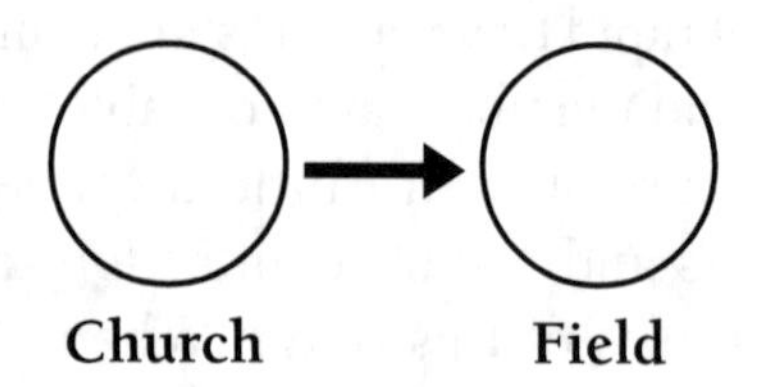

Church: "We'll do it ourselves."

But as with the traditional model, there are downsides, for with all that the local church gains, much is lost as well. By not availing itself of the agency's expertise and experience, a church may plunge into a work blind to the issues and pitfalls at every turn. Field ministry may suffer when churches fail to develop a coherent philosophy—or even know what to consider in devising a strategy. Most detrimental is the difficulty of producing a sustainable ministry without the broader resources of numerous churches, thereby leaving national partners in the cold when the ministry falters. Certainly the missions agency is not perfect in these regards, but there is every danger the local church will repeat the mistakes it has sought to avoid. One final caution: the churches most likely to attempt this direction are the larger, better-resourced congregations. The unfortunate implication, then, is that direct field involvement is not for the smaller church, which must continue in the traditional role of missions patron.

My own experience as a missions pastor reflects these problems. Convinced that greater focus leads to greater participation, our church adopted a people group in the Balkans, in part because an agency was planning to send missionaries to this newly opened country. When that placement fell through, our church teamed up with another PCA church to serve as our own sending agency. We recruited and selected candidates, provided pre-field training, helped the missionaries settle into the country, and worked with them closely as they developed a strategy. Our congregations enthusiastically supported them through their prayers, giving, and several short-term projects. Our missions leaders visited them two to three times a year and regularly communicated with them via email and phone. The actual ministry was busy and robust, providing a significant contribution to training emerging church planters. Based on the commitment from our churches and the vision on the field, everything seemed to be going great.

Over time, however, we saw that it was difficult to sustain the work. Policies and philosophy were created on the fly and in reaction to ever changing circumstances. We made strategic mistakes that could easily have been avoided had we more experience. The administration of funds and resources seemed a common distraction from "the real work." We didn't know what level of care and oversight was appropriate, including support for re-entry into the U.S. And with a limited pool of candidates, we ultimately could not provide successors to our missionaries. The work was essentially turned over to another mission agency, and our current involvement remains relatively insignificant.

A New Approach

There is, however, a third way. The unavoidable trend in missions today is for churches to connect directly to the field; this direction should be accepted and affirmed. The agency brings experience and facilitation for long-term ministry; this role should likewise be accepted and affirmed. A model for the future, then, is one that builds on the strengths of the two models mentioned above, while attempting to minimize the weaknesses. This new approach involves the creation of a partnership of all interested churches, the sending agency and field workers to develop and coordinate ministry related to a specific field.

The dominant message here is "We all need each other, so let's work together," as suggested by the following diagram:

Partnership

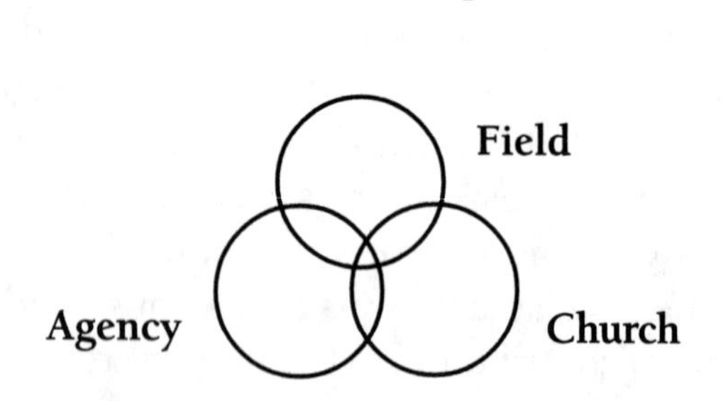

All: "Let's work together."

In this model, MTW becomes a facilitator of missions involvement, rather than the traditional "here's what we're doing" agency. In this facilitating role, MTW's first question to churches changes from "Will you join us?" to "Where has God called you to serve? And if you don't know, can we help you discover it?" A group of churches with a common focus would then partner together with MTW and missionaries to initiate and/or develop a work.

We are currently in the early stages of several such partnerships. After a formation period of defining how the various partners will work together, they are beginning to cooperate in ministry. One partnership is establishing an English lending library in Central Asia, collecting, cataloguing, and shipping the books, then sending interns to teach English and establish relationships. Another partnership is focusing on church-planter training, helping to develop the curriculum and materials. The essential difference in this model is the level of communication and interaction among the various partners.

Although each partner may contribute to any aspect of the partnership, it has been helpful to clarify which partners will take the lead in various responsibilities, as follows.

The field workers (missionaries and national leaders) determine ministry vision and strategy, carry out the ministry, and equip partners to effectively serve alongside. Churches provide input to field strategy, initiate projects with field approval, and participate in ministry. Further, they educate, equip and send members in missions, help provide financial support, and can assist in candidate assessment and training.

MTW continues its responsibilities to administrate financial accounts, assess and train candidates, and supervise the missionaries. It will also facilitate the partnership by fostering communication and coordination, and keeping the partnership on track by preventing both irrelevance (by not being engaged) and micromanagement (by dictating to the field). All the partners—field, church and agency—are responsible to promote the ministry, expand and organize the partnership, and recruit and care for team members.

A Great Attempt

Partnership in some expression is nothing new. What is different in this emerging model, however, is the combination of two elements: the high degree of interaction and coordination among the various partners, and the concentration of ministry on a particular work. It is premature and even hubristic to term this direction the "future of missions," but those involved to date have great hope that something truly significant is taking shape. They like being more connected to the field and to each other, and they see the potential to invigorate the missions ministry of both the local church and the overseas field. The ability of these first partners to see over the horizon recalls the faith that William Carey called his brothers to demonstrate.

The passage from Isaiah that Carey spoke from at the Nottingham conference challenges us to "enlarge the place of your tent, stretch your tent curtains wide." The surprise in this passage is not that we need to make room for the expansion of God's kingdom, but that we are to do so *before* the growth actually occurs. That requires faith, a deep conviction that God is going to work, and we need to get ready for it. These partnerships are a waste of time and energy if God has no place for us in the Great Commission. But if He does, partnering with others demonstrates faith by expanding our capacity to serve—even prior to seeing the fruit He will bring. May we too "expect great things from God; attempt great things for God."

__Rev. Scott Seaton__ has served as a missionary to Japan with MTW, as missions pastor at Intown Community Church, PCA, and now serves as the International Director of Enterprise for Christian-Muslim Relations at MTW.

A Partnership Story: Pinewood Presbyterian Church

Rod Whited

Our missions team and session were interested in helping local churches get planted. We believe the best way to penetrate a culture with Jesus Christ and the Bible is to plant local churches. Andrew Lamb, Partnership Consultant for Mission to the World, got us thinking about partnering with the MTW team and nationals in Mexico. Andrew did excellent groundwork for us, and suggested we consider the team in Monterrey, Mexico. We were interested in Mexico since it's our next-door neighbor and we were supporting two missionary families there.

But when I first heard about Monterrey, at a missions team meeting, I said, "I think the Baja Peninsula is too far away." Then I found out that Monterrey, a teeming city of over five million, was 146 miles south of McAllen, Texas. And we liked the idea of actually partnering with Mexican nationals through MTW.

In the summer of 1996, Jim Miller, a member of our missions team, was in San Antonio, Texas, when he and his wife took a bus to Monterrey to meet with Rich Wagner and Gary Watanabe, MTW missionaries serving in Monterrey at that time. Jim liked what he saw, and learned that Monterrey was a city in need of hundreds of local churches. Rich Wagner had a vision, a plan, and a great relationship with the nationals. In 1998, we entered a four-year agreement with MTW, the National Presbyterian Church of Mexico, and Carlos Cervantes, a local pastor. Our missions team chairman, Hal Wilkening, and Carlos Cervantes signed the partnership in front of our congregation, and the partnership began in earnest.

From the beginning, we approached the partnership with more than money. We prayed, publicized, and talked about our mission church in Monterrey. We began to show up in Monterrey. One of our couples attended Carlos and Adriana's wedding. When their twins were on the way, we had a huge baby shower at our church. Ruling elders visited Monterrey with MTW short-term teams or on vision trips. Three short-term teams have now been sent to build, to conduct VBS, and to help with evangelism.

One of our ruling elders, Al Couch, now seventy-one, fell in love with the Mexican people, and was called by God to assist Rich and Ramona Wagner (MTW Monterrey team leader), to help the other MTW missionaries, and to support and encourage the Mexican pastors. Al liked what he saw in the potential of many local churches being planted. He appreciated Rich Wagner's vision. He was introduced to Andres Garza, the Church Planting Coordinator for the National Presbyterian Church of Mexico (NPC) for Northern Mexico. Al Couch, now known on both sides of the border as "Monterrey Jack," has headed up several vision trips, taking ruling and teaching elders to Monterrey for them to see for themselves what God is doing in northern Mexico. Many of them are now partners.

In the last few years, in addition to the three missionary couples we were already supporting in Mexico, Pinewood has assumed support for a missionary couple and single missionary in Mexico and for two Mexican church planters. A young couple in our church, Jason and Eva Borko, have been accepted as short-term missionaries.

I believe Christians want to be part of something that is really making a difference for Christ. To be part of a church-planting movement is extremely satisfying as we see Christ's Great Commission being fulfilled. Partnering helps you focus on particular people and geography. It makes the missionaries real. It helps you to be personally involved.

In 1996, the people of Pinewood were contributing about $5,000 per year. We have now made a $250,000 commitment to be fulfilled over the next several years.

Partnering helps you to be personally involved over and above the money. In a partnership, it is not "them" and "us." It's all "us." That's the best part.

Rev. Rod Whited *is the senior pastor of Pinewood PCA in Middleburg, FL.*

Mission Ignition: Partnership in Ministry

CHUCK FROST

I serve a "missions-minded" church family. Westminster Atlanta, from its birth one hundred one years ago, has "prayed, given and gone" in response to the simple clarity of Christ's command to go and make disciples. What would cause Westminster's heart for missions to pound more deeply for this present generation?—*partnership*. The name implies the obvious—people working together to accomplish a goal.

This partnership model has ignited a new era of excitement and personal participation in missions for the Westminster family! Through our relationship with Turgay Üçal, executive director of the Turkic World Presbyterian Church, our partnership focus is on the Muslim world of Turkic-speaking peoples. This partnership, named Enterprise Turkey, directly connects Westminster and sister PCA churches with front-line ministry on the field. Enterprise Turkey (known as ET) enables the corporate power (prayer, money, and people) of a number of sister congregations to be more directly applied to a specific field of ministry. While a partnership is in fact assisted and encouraged both organizationally and administratively at the denominational level, the application of personal energy comes directly from the constituent church families. This produces both excitement and challenge.

The excitement is seen at Westminster in a clearer focus on a particular mission field rather than being so wide spread that we make personal connection with nothing. This more clearly focused pursuit produces genuine relationships with people on the field and thereby produces personal prayer and resource involvement, not to mention personal trips to the field. Our first vision trip shepherded four individuals to Turkey and Bulgaria. Upon their return, their excitement and interaction with peers produced a group of twelve for the next trip—with a waiting list. It is our hope that in the next ten years, at least 50% of the adults of Westminster will engage in a short-term missions trip. Our sister churches in ET have similar aspirations. Sister churches encouraging and challenging each other is another layer of this excitement. Suddenly, people in the pew see themselves as personally significant in Christ's redemptive plan.

But, the challenges are not insignificant. We are all on the same bus—a helpful metaphor—delighting in the renewed intimacy and involvement of partnering. Who is driving the bus? We must remember that our commitment is to assist national pastors in *their* work of making disciples (evangelizing and church planting). Great care must be taken to prevent the inertia of "American resources" from unintentionally blundering into the driver's seat. We must strive for a collegial relationship that supports and encourages rather than directs and demands. Effective partnership ministry is significantly rooted in the intimacy of direct involvement—confident to be partners, not patrons. Our goal is to promote kingdom growth. We are not bringing light to the darkness—we are bringing fuel for the light that already burns.

So why is the Westminster family so excited about this model for missions? Why is there a waiting list for our next vision trip to the Turkic world?

Here's the linkage:

- We develop deeper personal contact relationships with people on the field.
- We become more careful prayer warriors through those close relationships.

- We give more sacrificially where we have a heart investment.
- We are eager to go to help and encourage.

For Westminster Atlanta, partnership has ignited missions momentum. The bus is moving—jump on board!

Rev. Chuck Frost is the senior pastor of Westminster PCA in Atlanta, GA.

Partnership: A Heart Commitment

TURGAY ÜÇAL

The following is taken from an interview with **Pastor Turgay Üçal** of Istanbul Presbyterian Church. The TWPC [Turkic World Presbyterian Church] is partnering with a number of PCA churches in their efforts at church planting in the Turkic-speaking world.

Partnerships Are Partners Are People

This theme ran through the interview with Pastor Üçal concerning partnering—it's people that make or break a partnership. With twenty years of experience in partnering to one degree or another with believers from Turkey and abroad, Pastor Üçal has a broad base for commenting on partnering for the gospel.

A Number of Common Values Are Important for Any Partnership

He stressed the need for a core group of people within the partnership who are committed to investing in each other for the long-term. That doesn't disqualify short-term projects, but those projects need a group of people behind them who are committed to the long-term. Plans, strategies, focus areas for outreach, etc., are useful, but fall short without depth of relationships. Though this is true everywhere, it is even more important in such a heavily relational country as Turkey; it is investing in people that makes a partnership effective and long lasting.

That means time together. It means understanding and appreciating each other—our histories, cultures, current situations, hopes, and struggles. MTW's regional director for Central Asia quotes one of his former professors: "To understand is to stand under, which is why it's so easy to see why it ain't so easy to do."

It means praying to grow in our love for each other, and sharing our lives, including the trials and crises. It means confessing and repenting when we haven't loved well, and asking for the Father to change us. It's a supernatural work because of our constant tendency toward self-centeredness. It means serving with an attitude of humility, not as an "expert" with all the answers.

Pastor Üçal spoke of trust as well. This is the fruit of investing. Without trust, a partnership will not flourish. Ultimate trust is in the work of the Holy Spirit in each other's lives. That will give us the patience and hope to press on through difficult times.

He also mentioned the need for common goals. He believes another strength of our partnership is our mutual "heartbeat for church planting." Partners should agree on their goals. This means consistent and open communication between all involved. We need "active listening"—asking questions to make sure we understand correctly. It means not making quick judgments about each other's actions or motives, but taking the time to understand the hearts in a matter.

Flexibility is another important value. It's a willingness to hold our plans, our expectations, our schedules, and our cultural backgrounds with an open hand before the Father. "In his heart a man plans his course, but the LORD determines his steps" (Proverbs 16:9).

These are the values that should guide our partnerships. By God's grace, as we live out the gospel, we will see the results we desire. Here in Turkey, the church is gaining ground in having a hearing within the country. It's a long-term work. A strong partnership is the result of "loving God with all your heart, strength and soul; and your neighbor as yourself." It's not just an intellectual commitment, but a heart commitment as well. Let's pray that

God will continue to bring together partners who are committed to these values and goals.

***Rev. Turgay Üçal** is the pastor of the Istanbul Presbyterian Church in Istanbul, Turkey as well as the executive director of the Turkic World Presbyterian Church.*

Section IV—Mercy Ministry: Looking Compassionately

It Is the Gospel, in Mighty Word and Mighty Deed!

Randy Nabors

We have no new theology, only one as old as Isaiah, Jesus, and the book of James. We have no new theology, only one that doesn't get used as often as it should. We are believers in the Word of God, we have honored the gospel, and we did that by believing it. We found that it truly is the "power of God unto salvation." And in this gospel we also found the love of God. We have been loved by God through His people, and God has loved His people through us.

As those who are Reformed and evangelical, we have had to fight many battles with error. We have had to be tenacious about what truth is and where it comes from, and we have been diligent to articulate what we mean. We have often paid a price for such a stubborn commitment to what we believe is the only hope of future generations, that they not lose the certainty of the faith of their forefathers.

Sometimes in our battles we have not stressed all of the Word, especially when it was the Word itself that seemed to be at stake. Surely though, there never was a true Christian who did not in some faltering degree practice what the Word teaches, especially when it comes to love. When we have not loved, we have been inconsistent with what we have preached. All of the Word, the

Holy Bible, which we love, which is so powerful to save, which is complete and so clearly reveals the will of God, speaks so simply of being. It is the being that reveals what we are, not the knowing.

Living the Gospel

We have no need to attack the knowing part of our faith. It is truth that we need and which saves us. We are not attacking our intellectual understanding of the faith, just how essential it is for that knowing to have made a difference, in our being. So one could possibly be a missionary of the "knowing," and know a great deal for oneself, and be absolutely ineffective in reaping the harvest. One can, in fact, be absolutely a hindrance, even antithetical, to the mission of the gospel by knowing and letting others know we know it, but not living it.

It is the living of the gospel that God wants and that God uses. Certainly He could have given the world pages written from heaven, and dropped from the skies. Certainly He could have used technology to speak it, giving every man a set of headphones. For some reason God likes relationships, and so He sent His Son, by whom He has spoken to the world. We call this the incarnation, and there never has been such a deed to display the Word of God.

God loves the poor, and commissioned His Son and us to go to them. And we bring to the poor the Word, something that is preached. Bringing the Word to someone inevitably gets us involved in their lives, or else we really have not sought to disciple them, and so the Word becomes something that is lived. These two things—word and deed—can be intellectually split. We are even sophisticated enough, and wicked enough, to attempt to do one without the other. Yet, they are inseparable, for each validates the other.

How strange that we would plant churches that reflect our theological weakness, yes, even our hypocrisy. That we would plant churches of "knowers," and give them no vision, or leadership, or example of what it means to live out the gospel and love the brethren, and love the poor and do good to all men, or let our light shine before men so that they might see our good works and glorify our Father which is in heaven. So strange that we would fight a false theology of salvation by good works and not articulate, or model, a theology that shows we are saved unto good works that have been preordained that we should walk in them.

How strange that we should become veterans of a verbal and literary war over how much each other is right, and know so little about being right and doing good in the world. While proud of the scars we have for the battle over truth, should we be ashamed that we have so few scars in the doing of justice, the love of mercy, the sharing of our bread with the hungry, the clothing of the naked, and the visitation of the prisoners and the sick?

Can you see a vision of a missionary who knows what he believes, who is rock solid on the authority of the Word of God, who knows the gospel and knows how to teach it? He knows what it is, and what it isn't, and he learns how to put it in the language of the people to whom he goes so that they can understand it. And while he does this, he makes the widows heart to sing, he gives the orphan hope. He ministers Christ to the least of the brethren of Christ as he visits a woman dying of AIDS, builds an orphanage for her children, creates a home for children who sleep in garbage dumps at night, recruits a doctor to build a hospital, recruits a deacon to come and build an industry, trains a local pastor, not only in the Word but in the doing, and all the people begin to speak well of this thing in their midst. It is the gospel, in mighty word and mighty deed.

What would the world be like and how would it be shaken if holistic churches were planted in communities of need so that the things that are weak would confound the things that are mighty; and the base things and the things which are despised (the people God chooses) would bring to nothing the things that are: so that no flesh should glory in His presence?

***Rev. Randy Nabors** is senior pastor of New City Fellowship PCA in Chattanooga, TN.*

Word, Deed, and Presence: Displaying God's Splendor in a Broken World

Brian D. Riedel

[1] The Spirit of the Sovereign Lord is on me, because the Lord has anointed me to preach good news to the poor. He has sent me to bind up the brokenhearted, to proclaim freedom for the captives and release from darkness for the prisoners,
[2]to proclaim the year of the Lord's favor and the day of vengeance of our God, to comfort all who mourn,
[3]and provide for those who grieve in Zion—to bestow on them a crown of beauty instead of ashes, the oil of gladness instead of mourning, and a garment of praise instead of a spirit of despair. They will be called oaks of righteousness, a planting of the Lord for the display of his splendor. (Isaiah 61:1–3)

Marisol (not her real name) is a twenty-one-year-old Quechua woman who lives in the small village of Pallpanqay out-side of Cuzco, Peru. She grew up in a home characterized by extreme poverty, alcoholism, domestic violence, and instability as her father came and went from the household. Her relationship with her mother has been strained from childhood, no doubt due to the extreme survival pressures of their chaotic home, compounded by the burden and expense of Marisol's childhood illness. At the age of twelve years, Marisol first had seizures, which led to some initial inconclusive medical evaluation, a costly drain on the family's meager resources. Since that time, she continued to have alternating periods of greater and lesser seizure activity, with exacerbations commonly triggered by times of emotional stress. A related problem has been chronic and at times severe and disabling headaches.

Perhaps not surprisingly, as a teenager Marisol entered into a relationship with a physically abusive man prone to binge drinking, with whom she had her first child. When she was no longer able to tolerate his abuses, she moved on to a new, somewhat more tranquil liaison with her current partner, the father of her son. Unfortunately, in the grim reality of a stagnant economy in the developing world, her husband's employment has been spotty and inadequate to reliably provide for the family. What's more, there is ongoing bickering with her new in-laws who think poorly of Marisol, punctuated by sporadic appearances by her drunken and violent former partner to threaten and harass her.

When presenting to Mission to the World's Hinterlands health ministry for the first time for the evaluation of seizures and headaches, we met a somber, sad-appearing woman with little vitality and weighed down by a sense of hopelessness. We learned of her attempts at traditional remedies for her ills: she had tied several living frogs to her head with a towel and kept them there until they died three days later, though this had done little to relieve her headaches or seizures; similarly, drinking the warm blood of a newly-sacrificed black cat had not improved her energy or sense of well-being.

It might be tempting to rush to judgment or summarily dismiss what would seem to be primitive or barbaric elements in this biographical sketch, maintaining that a simple, clear proclamation of the gospel is all that is truly necessary to right what is wrong with this picture. However, as a missionary seeking to communicate the gospel cross-culturally and believing that it has the power to save in all cultures and in all brokenness of all times, the pivotal question one must ask is, *how* does the gospel speak into such a situation? In an effort to begin answering this question, it is useful to examine the channels through which God has made Himself known to us, namely through *word, deed,* and *presence*. Armed with such an understanding, we are better positioned to faithfully represent Him in this world.

One manner in which God reveals Himself to us is through His *Word*. This includes the Living Word, our Lord Jesus Christ, who embodies the most complete manifestation of the Godhead available to us. But it also includes the written Word, the Holy Scriptures, through which God has recorded and preserved His revelation for us through time. Most commonly perhaps, when we think of sharing the gospel with someone, our thoughts run to speaking words to them. Of course this is a necessary component of sharing the gospel, but at many times it may not be sufficient. In our contact with Marisol, imagine how hollow the words would ring if we merely exhorted her to "Keep warm and well fed" (cf. James 2:14 ff.), but did nothing to enter more fully into her struggles. Though one cannot fully share the gospel without proclaiming the name of Christ with words, neither can it be fully communicated ***only*** with words.

What, then, is lacking in a word-only expression of the gospel? Lacking is any convincing contact between theology and real life, possibly yielding hope for tomorrow, but offering little comfort, nor power for today. What results is a disembodied, theoretical spirituality of little use to a suffering person and with no ability to communicate the lavish, pursuing, redeeming, palpable love of our heavenly Father. What is needed is practical application of the gospel message to the here and now. This happens as a result of the gospel being lived out in the lives of the saints as it was always intended to be. It shows up as acts of mercy and service in a world of brokenness and need. As Dr. Timothy Keller[1] reminds us, mercy is a powerful apologetic for the gospel, which even a skeptical, unbelieving world is hard-pressed to overlook. Drawing once again from Marisol's experience, how much more credible would be a gospel that not only spoke healing *words* to her, but also ministered healing *actions* into her life in areas of physical need? Offering her wracked body a caring touch, pursuing accurate diagnosis, and effective medical treatment where previously she had received only indifference or antagonism from an impersonal health care system, investigating her husband's vocational potential and seeking to link him with job prospects so that he can more fully conform to his Creator's design for him as husband and father—and doing all this openly and unashamedly because of the love of Christ which dwells within us—how much more faithful a witness would that be to the fullness of the gospel truth of health, healing and wholeness available only in Christ?

It's evident, then, how a combined, balanced witness of word and deed more fully reflects the whole message of the gospel. But there's still another avenue by which our God chooses to make Himself known to us, and that is through His indwelling *presence* among us. Rather than merely issuing a judicial decree granting us righteousness as He might have done, God chose instead to send His Son who became flesh and made His dwelling among us (John 1:14). When He quickened our cold, stony hearts to first believe, it was through the person of His Holy Spirit moving within us. The simple fact is that God operates in individual lives, one at a time, to bring them into an intimate relationship with Himself. He has not left us as orphans; He has come to us (John 14:18).

So, then, it's not only through hearing the proclaimed *Word,* nor through *deeds* of mercy, but also through the nearness of our God to us through His indwelling *presence* that we are able to most fully and completely experience the gospel in our own lives. How appropriate it is, then, that our lives and our ministries should display the same well-rounded, full-bodied evidence to those with whom we seek to share Christ. On the practical plane, this translates into lives and ministries that are up close, personal, "hands in the dirt," highly relational, and with a tendency toward being low volume but very high touch. That's why, in the case of Marisol, it makes perfect sense to spend an hour or two of the extremely limited commodity of a missionary physician's time to merely be present with her, to sit in her humble adobe home, with a low, smoky eucalyptus fire popping in the corner of the dark room and with tonight's meal of guinea pigs still scurrying across the dirt floor and over the tops of one's shoes, listening carefully to her stories of pain, and thereby acknowledging that her story has not escaped the notice of a near and present God. By doing so, *we* more fully understand how to bring the truth of the gospel to bear in her life; by doing so, *she* comes to more fully risk trusting us to enter into the most broken corners of her life with that same gospel, and to risk believing that the One of whom we speak and whom we serve could possibly care for her.

We find reference to these concepts of word, deed, and presence in the text recorded in Isaiah 61, which our Lord Himself used to inaugurate His incarnational ministry (cf. Luke 4:18–19). According to this passage, Jesus sought to emphasize that the defining characteristics of His earthly ministry would include being sent to the brokenhearted and captives (i.e., being *present* among them), proclamation of freedom, release and favor (*word*) and binding up, comfort and provision (*deed*). As one reads through the whole of the gospel narrative, it is very evident how He operated in each one of these domains.

In word, deed, and presence, then, God reveals Himself to us. Similarly, in word, deed and presence we can more fully display the fullness of His character to those around us. For Marisol, we've seen that it means spending time with her, offering her medical attention, caring whether her children have food to eat and her husband work to do, and speaking words of truth to her from the Scriptures. We do it because we seek to be faithful witnesses to our God, and we want our testimony to be a high-fidelity reproduction of the gospel we've come to know, thereby displaying His splendor.

Marisol's life has taken a turn for the better. Her husband has been linked with nearly continuous employment, resulting in more regular income and food on the family table. Her once very troublesome in-laws have also been touched by ministry to their own acute medical needs, and are beginning to ask questions about the gospel and to examine their former treatment of her. Marisol's seizures were, in fact, found to be pseudo-seizures upon further careful investigation—a neurological manifestation of a deeply disturbed and wounded person. They have now virtually disappeared in the light of an ongoing, sustained interest in her well being from her brothers and sisters in Christ. The somber, lethargic desperate woman of a few months back now has a nearly continual smile on her face, and not simply a pasted-on Sunday School smile either, but rather the tranquil, radiant smile of a life more at rest in Christ. In the complexity of the brokenness that previously characterized her life, it's doubtful whether words or deeds or presence alone would have had the power to lift her from the mire. However, offered together as an integral testimony to the full character of our redeeming God, they are bringing beauty from ashes and the firstfruits of *shalom* wholeness in Christ.

***Dr. Brian Reidel**, a pediatric gastroenterologist, and his wife, Julie, are long-term missionaries in Peru.*

Acknowledgement

The author is indebted to Dr. Gary Waldecker and his monograph "Toward a Theology of Movement" for his illuminating exposition of the tri-fold self-revelation of God in word, deed, and presence.

1. Timothy J. Keller, Ministries of Mercy. *The Call of the Jericho Road,* 2nd Ed. (Phillipsburg, NJ: P&R Publishing, 1997), p. 107.

Helping the Helpless: Ministry to Street Children

Tom Stewart

Though my father and mother forsake me, the Lord will receive me. (Psalm 27:10)

Ministry to street children is an intensely personal business. It is difficult to deal in the abstract or merely philosophical when coming face-to-face with a child living on the street. Many, perhaps most of us, must grapple with a whole host of emotions when we first see this reality. We may feel shock and incredulity that families and societies would allow their children to be homeless, anger that so few seem to care, compassion for little ones suffering for the sins of their own parents, and even guilt for our own state of affluence and comfort. When the scope of the problem finally sinks in, we may be tempted to throw our hands up in despair. Perhaps we secretly feel a sense of relief in thinking that the problem is so overwhelming as to be insoluble. The issue is just too massive, too global, with too many roadblocks. What can one person do?

My own story with street children began in the early 1990s when a visiting missionary from Nairobi, Kenya, told me about the problem of street children there. She was overwhelmed and burdened by the large number of these children in the city. She wanted to help, but if she gave food to one, she was quickly surrounded by a hundred.

Her account was so vivid I was deeply moved. I knew that there were poor children in the world, but I had no idea that there were hordes of homeless kids growing up on the streets of major cities. I could not help but think of our own young children at the time. Could I rest, even for a moment, knowing that one of them was alone on the street?

Over the years, the memory of the missionary's description faded, but it never disappeared. About eight years later my wife and I met another couple planning a cross-cultural ministry to street children in a different part of the world. I began to learn that the problem of street children was not confined to a city, a country, or even a continent, but it was a global problem. A few months later, we participated in a trip to see street children firsthand. By the end of the week, God's call seemed undeniable.

Like almost everyone else, my initial understanding of the street child problem was simplistic and naïve. I began to read books, research web sites, and attend conferences. My outlook began to change with an understanding of the difficulties and complexities of working with street children. I was struck by the realization that there is no quick fix for this horrific problem.

These children are the victims of indifference, abandonment, and physical and sexual abuse. Regaining the trust of a victimized child is not easy. Healing emotional and spiritual wounds is always difficult, requiring a genuine loving and long-term commitment.

The Church Is Key.

I learned that there are perhaps hundreds of Christian ministries to street children in the world, but few are grounded in churches. As I looked at a variety of para-church ministries, a commitment grew into a strong conviction—that *the church is not just important to street child ministry, but foundational.* Children raised in the church are likely to continue in the church as adults. Children raised outside the church, even in otherwise

Christian settings, are usually not active, committed church members in their adult lives.

Another conviction grew that street children are not second-class citizens in God's economy. Should we desire any less for the homeless children that God entrusts to our care than for our own children? What *do* we want for our own children? We want our children to know Christ and to be committed to His Church. If street children cannot find a home in the church, they are homeless indeed.

Occasionally I am asked about the place of a ministry to street children in world missions. I believe there are at least four biblical reasons, beginning with the general context of mercy ministry:

First, mercy (or diaconal) ministry is effective for the spread of the gospel.

"So the word of God spread. The number of disciples in Jerusalem increased rapidly, and a large number of priests became obedient to the faith."

This account of remarkable church growth occurs in Acts 6:7, and immediately follows the choosing of the first diaconate. For the first time in the early church, there is a formal division of responsibility between word and deed, and the results were profound. Was it the preaching of the Word by the apostles or the public deed ministry to the widows (and probably others in need) that God used to cause this growth? I believe it was both.

Consider this observation from Dr. Tim Keller in *Ministries of Mercy*, p. 106–107:

> *Mercy has an impact. It melts hearts. It removes objections. It forces respect out of even those hostile to the gospel. Our good deeds glorify God in the eyes of the world (Matt. 5:16). Our concrete deeds of love for one another are an apologetic for the validity of the Christian faith "By this all men will know that you are my disciples, if you love one another" (John 13:35).*

True godly compassion to those in need is a powerful witness to an unbelieving world. The planting of national churches committed to word and deed is not only biblically balanced, but also, in God's providence, a formula for church growth.

Second, children are special in God's sight.

Jesus wanted children to have unhindered access to him (Matthew 9:14a), and warned of the direst consequence for anyone who would cause a child to sin (Mark 9:12). He said that welcoming a single child in his name was the same as welcoming the Father (Luke 9:48). He openly showed affection for children and blessed them (Mark 10:16). Jesus even said that the kingdom of heaven belongs to those sharing a spiritual likeness to children (Luke 18:16). Among many references in the Old Testament, God ordains praise from infants and children (Psalm 8:2), who are to be taught the fear of the Lord (Psalm 34:11). For parents, children are a spiritual heritage and a reward (Psalm 127:3). Spiritual instruction of children as the next generation (who are in turn then to teach their children) is a priority in Scripture (Deuteronomy 4:9).

Third, children are not excluded from the Great Commission.

The nineteenth-century evangelist, Dwight L. Moody, once preached a crusade in which he said, there were "two and a half" converts. When asked the age of the child who had become a Christian (the "half" convert), he corrected the questioner by saying that he was speaking of *two children* and *one adult*. The adult's life, Moody explained, was half over, while the children had their whole lives ahead of them. Children are whole people, indeed.

In the Great Commission (Matthew 28:16–20), Jesus commands us to "go and make disciples of all nations, baptizing . . . and teaching them to obey everything I have commanded you." The last phrase is reminiscent of Psalm 78:5: "He decreed statutes for Jacob and established the law in Israel, which he commanded our forefathers to teach their children . . ."

Proverbs 22:6 tells us to "train a child in the way he should go, and when he is old he will not turn from it." I believe the biblical mandate is clear. Children should be trained as disciples. While the Great Commission is for people of all ages, certainly children should be included in our missionary endeavors.

Fourth, care of the orphan and fatherless is God's plan.

Prominent in the book of Deuteronomy are numerous references to the "fatherless," especially in regard to God's concern for them and our responsibility for their care:

> *He defends the cause of the fatherless and the widow, and loves the alien, giving him food and clothing.* (Deuteronomy10:18).

> *When you are harvesting in your field and you overlook a sheaf, do not go back to get it. Leave it for the alien, the fatherless and the widow, so that the Lord your God may bless you in all the work of your hands.* (Deuteronomy 24:19)

The passage from Zechariah 7:9–10 is particularly poignant, since street children are not only fatherless, but also poor and alien:

> *This is what the Lord Almighty says: "Administer true justice; show mercy and compassion to one another. Do not oppress the widow or the fatherless, the alien or the poor . . ."*

In a well-known New Testament passage James states that:

> *Religion that God our Father accepts as pure and faultless is this: to look after orphans and widows in their distress and to keep oneself from being polluted by the world.* (James 1:27)

Personal holiness and acts of mercy, the apostle says, are not alternatives to choose between, but complimentary evidences of a genuine faith. Anything less, he implies, is impure and faulty religion in God's sight.

Coming Full Circle

In a sense, ministry to street children brings us full circle in our Christian lives. We all begin as children, physically helpless and spiritually orphaned. God reaches us in our helplessness ("I will not leave you orphans," Jesus said in John 14:18), redeems us through no merit of our own, and prepares us to do good works for His glory (Ephesians 2:10). He offers us, through His Church, the privilege of serving others in their helpless condition.

In Matthew 25:42–45, Jesus makes this troubling pronouncement:

> *For I was hungry and you gave me nothing to eat, I was thirsty and you gave me nothing to drink, I was a stranger and you did not invite me in, I needed clothes and you did not clothe me, I was sick and in prison and you did not look after me. They . . . will answer, "Lord, when did we see you hungry or thirsty or a stranger or needing clothes or sick or in prison, and did not help you?" He will reply, "I tell you the truth, whatever you did not do for one of the least of these, you did not do for me."*

It is difficult to image one more "least" than an abandoned, abused, and homeless child. Contrary to a popular saying, God does not help those who help themselves—why would he need to? God helps the helpless. Should not we as well?

***Dr. Tom Stewart** left a medical practice in Gainesville, GA to found and direct StreetChild Mission International of MTW.*

The Crisis of AIDS and the Church's Response

DEBORAH DORTZBACH

Anastasia

The pencil thin body of Anastasia stretched before me, bathed in her urine-soaked bed. Her sunken eyes met mine as I squeezed her raging hot hands.

"Please," she said, in a barely audible mumble. "Take me to the hospital."

". . . but Anastasia," I answered, "I don't think they will accept you. There are not enough beds."

"Please, please!" she said. "I want to go."

It was her dying wish.

I struggled to express why I knew it would be better if she stayed at home, near her children and with her neighbors nearby to support her. Each time I tried to put into words the reality that she was dying and she needed to be near her children, her church friends gathered around and said, "Oh no, you can't tell her she is dying. You can say anything else, but you can't tell her that." In their minds, to talk about death, is to bring it to reality. No one in the worldview of African traditional religion wants to be the harbinger of death.

Yet, Anastasia *was* dying of AIDS. I knew that. It didn't used to be like this. In almost thirty years in Africa, working in famine camps in Ethiopia, cholera wards in Eritrea, and child-care clinics under trees in eastern Kenya, this epidemic leaves me weaker and more desperate than any other health crisis I have faced.

Anastasia's real risk was not being born in Sub Sahara Africa and living in urban slums with terribly inadequate health care. Her *real* risk to AIDS was her unfaithful husband, who had preceded her in death. It is a behavior issue not a poverty or medical issue.

Her story may be repeated millions of times over. "Since the epidemic began, more than sixty million people have been infected with the virus. HIV/AIDS is now by far the leading cause of death in Sub-Sahara Africa, and the fourth-biggest global killer."[1] Among eighty-eight countries studied by a combined group of the Joint United Nations Programmes on HIV/AIDS, 13.4 children under the age of fifteen have already lost a mother, father, or both parents to AIDS. By 2010, we can expect up to twenty-five million.[2] In real terms that means AIDS is no longer a stranger to us—many of us know personally someone who has died

The Real Issues

Behavior

To get to real issues in the AIDS crisis, we have to address misconceptions. AIDS is not primarily a problem of physical sickness, though that is usually where we spend most of our money, time, and energy. It is not about poverty. AIDS is about behavior—sexual behavior. It is a more formidable task to change behavior than to discover medical formulas for cures.

Beliefs

Behavior springs from beliefs. Deeply rooted in African traditional belief is the problem of curses. AIDS acts like a curse, because it is insidious, cannot be fully explained, even scientifically. It has no cure and can affect anyone.

Christians sometimes simplistically claim persons with AIDS are paying for their sins. Some feel God especially condemns sexual sin, which is extended to the "sin of AIDS."

All these beliefs breed fear, isolation, apathy, and a culture of silence around HIV/AIDS. It is a silence that has to be broken by all of us in the Americas, Africa, Asia, and Europe.

Our Obstacles

AIDS Is Big, and It Affects Everyone

In the 1970s we made great progress with childhood diseases and health issues. In the 1990s we buried many of those children, now young adults in their prime of life struck down by HIV/AIDS. Life expectancy is falling in most countries in Africa. Average life expectancy in Sub Sahara Africa is now forty-seven years when it would have been sixty-two years without AIDS.

Unless trends change, children born today in southern Africa have a life expectancy of fifteen to twenty years (*Healthy*, 2000). Our advances in child health are threatened as children succumb to HIV themselves or are faced with severe shortages of primary health care, education, or basic needs. Many who survive early childhood will be orphans.

Lack of Global Political Will and Priorities

Few nations admit the severity of the problem, and most fail to do what they could to stem the global tide. Without addressing AIDS as a national and global priority, other priorities such as national security, economic and political stability, and the provision of basic services such as education and health may not be met.

Lack of Resources

AIDS is not a poor man's disease, but the impact on the poor is devastation. AIDS is hitting where resources are minimal, creating a vicious spiral of deepening poverty and a reduction in the pool of human resources. Household assets in Africa are often consumed as families search for cures, both biomedical and traditional. In

Zimbabwe today, two teachers need to be trained for every one dying of AIDS just to keep schools open.

The resource of the extended family is usually the social safety net to assist the nuclear family with those who are sick, family finances, and the care for orphans left behind. It is not uncommon for an elderly grandmother to have the sole responsibility of caring for all of her grandchildren because her own children have all died of AIDS.

At the same time, governments are faced with choices concerning the allocation of limited healthcare resources. Political pressure is mounting for inclusion of anti-retroviral drugs, but even simple antibiotics are unaffordable by many, and people like Anastasia struggle to find twenty cents to get to the clinic.

AIDS Is in Our Church

One of the tragedies of this epidemic is that AIDS is strong in our most evangelized, not least evangelized countries. Africa has the fastest growing church in the world and bears the brutal brunt of the global burden of AIDS.

While many pew warmers are not bedroom defilers, none can claim purity. The scarlet "A" may not be on our chests, but it's in our hearts. This is not new to God. He went to such an extreme to show us our desperate condition, He told the prophet Hosea to marry prostitution itself. "Go take yourself an adulterous wife and children of unfaithfulness because the land is guilty of the vilest adultery *in departing from the Lord*" (Hosea 1:2).

We may or may not be HIV-positive, but we must understand how sin-positive we *all* are. That means in the context of this epidemic we *all* are called to serious reflection, conviction, confession, reconciliation, and action.

Our Opportunities

Protection: Moving from Belief to Action

Rwanda, just a few short years after genocide and war left the country bleeding and grieving, faces a more sustained and deadly struggle—the HIV/AIDS crisis. It is now hitting one in five people nationwide leaving many children orphaned twice—once from war and now from AIDS. Churches gathered in 1997 and again in 1998, determined not to allow yet another crisis to engulf them. They spoke boldly and committed to changing "belief to action and apathy to care" (*Declaration*, 1998).

Every woman in Kenya and other parts of Africa, has the multipurpose *kanga* wrap which she uses every day. A primary use is wrapping it around the waist to protect your clothing. When I first went to Kenya, I was given a *kanga* and went out to the fields to harvest with the other women. By noon I was exhausted, withered, and full of dust with only a handful of beans to show for a morning's work. We all took off the *kanga*, however, and entered the house with clean dresses. The *kanga* had done the work of protection.

Following God's Word protects families in the AIDS crisis. We know that, we preach that, but rarely do we equip each other to wrestle with the obstructions to obeying God's Word which our environments and sometimes our families breed.

Our youth probably do not need more preaching to help protect them. They need us to listen, dialogue, understand the environment and changing cultures they face, model godly roles in marriage and family, and encourage them to support each other in making wise choices.

Our churches need materials to help open dialogue into sensitive areas such as family roles, sexual health, communication, and godly leadership.

Support: Moving from Complacency to Care

The *kanga* is also often used by African mothers to carry their babies. Just as these babies are securely cared for, so those affected by AIDS need comfort and support, often to be carried. Providing this support is one of the greatest opportunities for the Church to personify the meaning of Christian families

We need "tried and true" methodologies of clinics, providing food and medicines, visiting the sick, and comforting families in their loss. But we also need to think much, much bigger if the church worldwide is going to make a difference. We must build partnerships, consciously avoiding past mistakes of isolationism and paternalism. The local church must be the focal point for support into the community through families in the church. We need more ideas born of local thought, grassroots solutions which can be maintained by the church, not by infusions of people or money from other regions.

Advocacy: Moving from Apathy to Compassion

Weekly African markets turn lonely, dusty villages into vibrant mega centers of activity, commerce, and color. There are always clusters of women surrounding banks of bright strips of cloth. The *kanga* attract attention, drawing eyes and pocketbooks toward their varied designs, colors, and printed proverbs. In the same way, AIDS needs advocacy—attention attracted to the right approaches, interventions, and solutions. The Church has those solutions in God's Word, but instead of holding high God's truth of obedience with compassion and mercy, we often push the challenge aside, even trampling on opportunity. Instead of being leaders in the global fight against AIDS, we lag at the end of the pack, pointing self-righteous fingers and mired in ecclesiastical debates.

To do this, we need collaboration between churches, not competition. A number of groups seek to foster collaboration including the Evangelical Alliance of South Africa, which gathers churches from all denominations together in community meetings to focus for one week on issues affecting their community. We also have much to learn from the courage and creativity of churches, individuals, and institutions that are involved in AIDS ministry, in as disparate places such as Cambodia, Malawi and Kenya.

One example is an institute that the Nairobi Evangelical Graduate School of Theology has started. It is an informal learning center to grapple more deeply with these problems facing Africa. The goal is to better expose and equip church leaders to address the issues, obstacles, and opportunities such realities as AIDS present. Known as the Institute for the Study of African Realities, it is a campus within a seminary campus for study, reflection, and interaction with other grassroots leaders, as well as scholars from across the African continent. This training model turns insufficient answers into deeper questions and looks beyond books to experience.

Conclusion

As the HIV/AIDS global crisis deepens in Africa and moves eastward with even greater vengeance to Asia, our challenge in medical missions will be to avoid returning to old strategies of doing for, rather than with, of creating institutions rather than building people, of focusing on international organizations rather than the local church. In our response to help, we must be cautious not to create models that are highly dependent on outside funding and limiting in scope, such as building high tech clinics and orphanages. Our challenge will be to strengthen people, not programs, direct people into movements, not just projects, and be committed to sharing ideas and resources rather possessing them.

How must the Church respond to the global crisis of AIDS? By sharing and demonstrating the message of Hosea 3:1, "Then the Lord said to me, 'Go show your love to your wife again, though she is loved by another and is an adulteress, love her as her Lord loves . . .'"—one Anastasia at a time.

Mrs. Deborah Dortzbach and her husband, Karl, have served as missionaries in Africa since 1980.

Article taken from presentation at "A New Rx for Medical Missions" conference at Wheaton College, October 2001. Used by permission.

Bibliography

Hunter, S., Williamson, J. (2000). *Children on the Brink.*

Declaration by Rwandan Church Leaders. (1998, November 2)

Healthy Life Expectancy. (2000). WHO

Report on the Global HIV/AIDS Epidemic. June 2000. (2000). Geneva, Switzerland: UNAIDS

1. *Report on the global HIV/AIDS epidemic*, 2002, UNAIDS, p. 44
2. *Children on the Brink 2002: A Joint Report on Orphan Estimates and Program Strategies, p. 3*

Section V—LOOKING AHEAD

Haystacks and Batons: A Seasoned Leader Looks to the Next Generation

JOHN KYLE

Leadership has been the subject of many books and much teaching. It has also been accurately said that one is not a leader unless he has followers.

In Christian organizations, one seldom refers to the person they report to as their "boss." We refer to that person often as the one we work beside or the one we work along with. But ultimately, the person leading the work, and set aside by those with authority to lead, is responsible for the accomplishment of the mission of the organization.

In thinking about the future leadership of missions, it is helpful to first look at the history of world missions. Many leaders helped pave the way for the further fulfillment of the Great Commission that Jesus Christ set out for us as believers. I believe Matthew 28:18–20 marked the course for us when Jesus Christ told His disciples:

> *"All authority in heaven and earth has been given to Me. Therefore, go and make disciples of all nations, baptizing them in the name of the Father and the Son and of the Holy Spirit, and teaching them to obey everything I have commanded you. And surely I am with you always, to the end of the age." In Acts 1:8, Jesus Christ's last words to His disciples as He left earth for heaven were, "But you will receive*

power when the Holy Spirit comes on you; and you will be my witnesses in Jerusalem, and in all Judea and Samaria, and to the ends of the earth."

Here we have clearly stated for us exactly what we are to do in the proclamation of the gospel and the boundless geography of that proclamation.

One of the first Protestant world missions leaders was Count Nicolaus Ludwig von Zinzendorf (1700–1760), founder of the Moravian Movement. He was raised in the home of aristocratic German nobility with its roots in the Holy Roman Empire. At the age of ten, he determined that his lifelong purpose would be to preach the gospel of Jesus Christ throughout the world. From the age of ten to sixteen, Zinzendorf studied in the Paedagogium in Halle, Germany. He had an unusual influence on his fellow students because of his life lived openly for Christ. With five other boys, he formed The Order of the Grain of Mustard Seed, which was a spiritual secret society whose members were bound together in prayer. Their purposes were evangelism, discipleship, and overseas missionary work. Thus, as a student, Zinzendorf took his first steps to spread the gospel worldwide. After founding the Moravian Movement in Germany, he began to send missionaries to the West Indies in 1722, and eventually, hundreds of missionaries were sent out to serve overseas by the Moravian Church. It has been written that the modern worldwide missionary movement was actually born in the hearts of a group of students, who joined together at Halle to pray for world evangelization.

Turning to America, it is little known that until 1812, missionaries did not have an agency to send them overseas. They would go under an agency in England or other countries of Europe. The genesis of such an agency in America began in 1806 when a group of students at Williams College in Massachusetts had a concern for the spiritual welfare of their fellow students. Led by Samuel Mills, who was sought after by other students because of his close walk with Christ, they began to spend Wednesday and Saturday afternoons in prayer with other students along the Hoosack River near the college. In August 1806, Mills and four other students were caught in a rainstorm while returning from their prayer meeting and took cover under a haystack in the field to wait out the storm. Their prayer while waiting focused on awakening an interest among their fellow students for the cause of foreign missions. Mills directed their discussion and prayer toward their own missionary obligation, and they formed the watchword, "We can do this if we will." The "Haystack Prayer Meeting" became a symbol of the awakening, student-driven impetus to world missions.

In June 1810, Samuel Mills and several fellow students attended the annual meeting of the General Association of Congregational Churches in Bradford, Massachusetts and presented a petition requesting the formation of a society that could send them overseas as foreign missionaries. On June 28th, their petition was officially received, so on June 28, 1810, it was recommended that the association begin a Board of Commissioners for Foreign Missions and come up with a plan to promote the spread of the gospel overseas. On February 19, 1812, Adoniram Judson and Samuel Newell and their wives sailed for India, and five days later Samuel Nott, Gordan Hall and Luther Rice sailed on another ship to India. Within four years of the Haystack Prayer Meeting, college students had been influential in the formation of the first North American missionary society, and a year-and-a-half later, the first missionaries were on their way to Asia.

I had the privilege of working with William Cameron Townsend, the co-founder of Wycliffe Bible Translators. He was a student at Occidental College in California where he attended chapel services regularly. He once told me that one chapel speaker was John R. Mott, the leader of the Student Volunteer Movement. At the close of Mott's moving message, Cameron turned to his friend, Louie Evans, who was sitting beside him, and said, "Louie, I believe God wants me to become a missionary!" Louie, who eventually became the senior pastor of the Hollywood Presbyterian Church, replied, "Cam, you do that and I'll support you!" (The Student Volunteer Movement sent out over twenty thousand career missionaries from its formation in 1888 to 1920. Their motto was "The Evangelization of the World in this Generation.")

My own experience with youth leads me to surmise that many of the future leaders of world missions are college graduates or are presently attending college. However, many will not reach the mission field until they are twenty-five to thirty years of age. They will take up to ten years to build their leadership skills, placing them at age thirty-five to forty when they assume top leadership positions.

In talking to people today who are engaged with students involved in college or Bible college training, I have learned that the commitment for long-term service is generally not great. There is a tendency for such youth to go on a short-term mission trip and feel that such service fulfills their need for missionary service overseas. My experience with the Millennium Generation, however, is hopeful that these young people have the commitment to serve Christ and they feel they can "make a difference" in our world for His glory.

When I was in Washington, D.C., a year ago, I met an emerging young leader who had just attended a meeting of young leaders where they were given a baton and told by older leaders, "We are passing the baton to you." The young leader held out his baton and said, "We young leaders do not want older leaders to pass batons to us! What we want is for them to come alongside of us and help us, not leave us." Then he shared how the leader of a Christian organization had given him office space in the organization's office and allowed him to use the office equipment as a means of encouraging him and coming alongside of him.

I recently participated in a meeting in Dallas called by Mission America, an organization involved in the evangelization of North America. The meeting was for the purpose of considering an alliance of organizations interested in training young Christian leaders and to consider sharing training materials and working together to further the training of young leaders between the ages of eighteen to thirty-five. Some of the information shared in small groups and discussed in open sessions was revealing as to the characteristics that make up many young leaders today, ages eighteen to thirty-five, often called the buster generation. The strength, which characterizes these young people is that, when they are given an opportunity, many are succeeding as leaders with boundless energy and unlimited potential.

These young leaders are highly relational with a pioneering spirit, and are generally dissatisfied with the status quo. They are also bold concerning what they consider as truth. Some of the weaknesses they face are the church structures and mature leaders who hold them back from adapting new paradigms. The younger leaders often have underdeveloped purposes, vision, and destiny. They also lack funding to develop programs. The opportunities that the church faces with these young leaders is to be assertive in developing and equipping them and in beginning to mentor them at a young age. There is also a great need to provide them with training, that is informal or hands-on. The threats they face are a lack of in-depth theological thinking or becoming anti-intellectual and lacking the full empowerment from older leaders. Moral impurity, which can evidence itself at any age, is a significant temptation and prevalent slayer of these young leaders. Finally, we have a poor system to identify emerging Christian leaders.

As I observe young Christian people, ages eighteen to twenty-five years of age, I note a genuine desire to serve Christ. They want to step out into the unfamiliar and unknown and trust Christ with His direction and protection, being obedient to what they know of the Scripture and open to learning. Upon these characteristics, leaders are formed, and in my opinion, there will be no dearth of mission leadership in the near future.

We older Christian leaders with missions experience, along with our local churches, must effectively utilize the giftedness of the younger generation in significant ways to achieve our common goal of reaching the lost of our world with the Good News. Thereby all praise and honor will go to Jesus Christ to the glory of God!

***Rev. John Kyle**, a former missionary to the Philippines, with his wife, Lois, has served two terms as Coordinator of Mission to the World, and between those terms, was vice-president of InterVarsity Christian Fellowship. He is presently the vice-president of the Evangelical Fellowship of Mission Agencies (EFMA).*

The Next Generation, the Church, and Missions

Bill Boyd

Being asked to write about "The Next Generation, the Church, and Missions" is kind of like being asked where the fish are and how to catch them. The temptation is to focus on equipment and strategy, lures, rods, reels, boats, motors, depth finders, hats, shirts, waders, sunscreen, scales, and limits. Now, don't get me wrong, all fishing involves some of these items, and good preparation often leads to good results. But it is possible to catch many fish and miss the true beauty and glory of fishing—which includes fellowship, reveling in the beauty of God's creation, and eating trout meuniere.

Perhaps evangelism and missions can be approached in much the same manner as fishing—even Jesus used the analogy. In our time and in our country, the emphasis in evangelism and missions seems to be pretty heavily on the gear, with much time and money spent on luring people to Christ Jesus and His Church. This is not inappropriate, but as one who is a part of and who works with "the next generation," I must report that oftentimes something smells fishy.

The current rage among postmoderns over authenticity derives in part from children of the Church who have observed and taken part in "fishing trips" that were high on gear and low on fish. These expeditions were all for the pursuit, but lacking in wonder over the pursued; big on quantity and size and indifferent to quality of species or environment. It is reminiscent of the portable "trout fishing" ponds that get hauled from mall to mall around the U.S. These fish have seen this bait before, seem to have little hunger or drive, and probably have no other viable options. At best, they are interested in the parade of bait the same way Holly Golightly was interested in Tiffany's—nice to dream about, but unrelated to reality. Further, very few real fishermen have an interest in "mall fishing." The prettiest and best-eating fish are the ones that are difficult to find and tend to put up a decent fight, and they don't come to you so much as you seek them out.

Having waded far enough into this analogy, let us do the same with a section of scripture that applies to the topic at hand, asking ourselves, "What might we learn from God's Word regarding 'The Next Generation, the Church, and Missions?'" Here is the scripture:

> *Then the eleven disciples went to Galilee, to the mountain where Jesus had told them to go. When they saw Him, they worshiped Him; but some doubted. Then Jesus came to them and said, "All authority in heaven and on earth has been given to Me. Therefore go and make disciples of all nations, baptizing them in the name of the Father and of the Son and of the Holy Spirit, and teaching them to obey everything I have commanded you. And surely I am with you always, to the very end of the age."* (Matthew 28:16–20, NIV)

One striking feature of "The Great Commission" is that it is set in a context of worship: "When they saw Him they worshiped Him, but some of them doubted." Evangelism and missions begin where worship begins, in the Church, with God's people. Without a doubt, the number one reason the world is confused about the Church is that the Church is confused about the Church. Doubt abounds concerning the Scriptures, Jesus, and the reality of the fall. Quite often, the only thing churchgoers fail to doubt is their own doubt. This text reminds us that doubt and confusion are not new to the Church. Churches that truly connect with next-generation Christians and pagans *will be the churches that first, like the blind man in*

Mark 8, admit that they have a sight problem. The world already knows that the Church has such a problem. It is just waiting on us to admit it.

Second, churches that reach the next generation will be *churches who clearly, boldly, consistently, repetitively, and humbly worship Jesus as the One who has "all authority in heaven and earth," given to him by His Father.* Why? Not because such is a magic mantra, but because worshipping in a consistently Christ-centered, biblical manner is supernatural and thus, totally counter-cultural; it is evidence of the Holy Spirit at work in the Church. It is "authentic" in the truest sense of the word, and people sense such when they come in contact with it. Everyone has a gimmick, but only one group has a sovereign God who has drawn near.

As a corollary to the above, when the Church becomes fascinated with the *all*-powerful nature of Jesus, then making disciples of *all* nations seems not only reasonable, but inevitable. "Teaching them to obey *all* I have commanded you" replaces a worldly strategy of "the minimum to the maximum, as fast as possible." Then the Church goes forth, resting in the reality that Jesus is with us "*always*," which means that only then does the Church go forth with true peace, that which the world hates, envies, and yearns for, all at the same time.

Such an approach to life flows from a settled belief that Jesus is good and He is in control of *all* things. The Westminster Confession and Catechisms refers to such as God's providence, a providence that is not a heartless doctrine, but the consequence of being a part of the family of the Most High. In other words, the next generation of the church will be just like the past generations. All of the good action will be where the truest and highest Christologies are found and where, in particular, such doctrines produce doxology.

Also striking in Matthew 28 is not only how, but *that* Jesus commands the disciples to baptize other disciples in the name of the Father, Son, and Holy Spirit. In a culture and church enamoured with productivity, baptism seems extraneous, especially if it is "merely symbolic." Why bother? Because He said so. Why did he say so? Because baptism symbolizes cleansing, the outpouring and blessing of the Holy Spirit; baptism gives us a new name. And because symbols are important. Baptism is a sacrament, a symbol connecting the giver and the receiver, a means of grace that is ultimately beyond explanation, especially when it is in the name of the Triune God. This is true mystery, grounded in the personality and work of the Godhead.

The coming generation acknowledges the reality of mystery, they just deny the true Mystery and the true nature of that mystery. There is little hope of reaching them if the Church fails to uphold her own, Christ-commanded rites. People don't abandon anything. We replace the things we abandon with something else. The Church must call unbelievers to replace their supposed mysteries with the worship of the living God, the God who unites us mysteriously with Himself in Christ Jesus by the power of the Holy Spirit. How many supposedly evangelical movements in America have emphasized a biblical theology of baptism? Why then, does it surprise us that the pagans consider the Church to be out of touch with reality? Why then does it surprise us when the children of the Church seem more attached to cultural symbols than Christian symbols? If we are sheepish (read "doubtful") of our own rites, why should others abandon theirs? And, when the Church upholds her rites, participating in them consistently, even frequently, and illumining them via the Word, the results are quite efficacious.

I had a conversation with a student about "raves," giant warehouse parties with multiple bands and multiple "effects," from tinted lights to LSD. We concluded that one thing that drew people to raves was the opportunity to get caught up in a performance that allowed one to relax, get into the music, and not worry about normal life pressures. I asked him, "Do you ever worry about whether or not the band will perform well or whether not you will perform well?" "No," he said, looking curious. I responded, "as convoluted as it may sound, that is a picture of the Church and Christ. Christ has performed and continues to perform on our behalf, and He catches us up in His act and frees us to deal with life as it really is, because the pressure is on Him, not us. The result is not escape, but true engagement of reality." This child of the Church was still looking to the world for symbols and a story in which to get caught up. To him, the symbols and story of the Scriptures were out of touch with reality, something that his experience had challenged very little.

If we want people to take the Bible seriously, then we must interpret it and apply it according to its own norms. Jesus gives us, among other things, a hermeneutical reminder here. Do not miss the forest for the trees. Do not forget the goal—restored communion with the one true God, the triune God, to His glory. The church that emphasizes the knowability and inscrutability of the Trinity is a church that says to the world, "We want to have our sense of reality deepened through our contact with mystery and our sense of mystery deepened through our contact with reality." After all, this is what the cross of Christ does for us and in us.

Finally, the verbs in this passage tell it all: going, making, bathing (baptizing), teaching, obeying. This is the stuff of normal, daily life, or at least it would be, if sin did not get in the way. Christianity went worldwide through the normal, daily things of life. Anyone can get fired up at a retreat, but to deal with the daily tasks of life with the fruit of the Spirit is truly counter-cultural. In other words, Jesus implicitly points us to a biblical world and life view as the context for disciple-making.

Finally, though Jesus does not mention it here, the book of Acts shows us Jesus' goal: the constitution of a new family, a new community called the church. The hunger for true community would be difficult to overemphasize as an attribute of the current and coming generation. Students talk about the desire to connect with others, about the desire to be part of something that imparts life, a sense of belonging, of friendship and family. The only way the Church will reach the coming generation is by taking its interfamily relationships seriously, with the joy that comes from the gospel of grace. People respond to the Church when they see church people taking others seriously and themselves with a grain of salt. When the mutual submission of the Godhead becomes evident in the Church, people respond. This new community also reminds us that mercy ministry is at the heart of church life, and is the undergirding of evangelism and missions. When the world sees the church as a haven for broken people, broken people start showing up at church.

The aforementioned simply involves taking seriously the basic things entrusted to the church. It means acknowledging, as William Willimon says, "people actually get saved through the Church."[1] It means trusting in the LORD with all of our hearts and not leaning upon our own understanding, acknowledging Him in our ways that He might make our paths straight. Nothing could be less popular and more attractive and effective at reaching the next generation and equipping them to serve.

The current rediscovery of biblically-based, content-rich, historically-informed worship is an encouraging sign that God's Spirit is at work, reaching and equipping the next generation. The emphasis on the Church as a body, a body that must act as the *family* of God, "teaching, rebuking, correcting, and training" one another with God's Word, is encouraging as well. Perhaps what we need most is a rediscovery of the Holy Spirit as the lifegiver, the One who equips God's people with a tone (fruit) that is altogether different than what the world has to offer. It results in an offensive rather than a defensive posture and produces in God's people a hunger that will stop at nothing in order to receive and impart true righteousness—in Christ. Could it be that the next generation, at home and abroad, will see a reshaping of the church in such a way that the old truths are rediscovered, repackaged, and replayed? And with the result that the gospel of grace in word and deed is in tune with historic Christianity, yet fresh with contemporary innuendo.

__Rev. Bill Boyd__ is the Reformed University Ministries campus minister at the University of Texas in Austin.

1. Willimon's book, *What's Right with the Church*, is a wonderful antidote to simple church criticism and a reminder that when the church keeps the main things the main things, the church and the culture get transformed.

Framing the Future

Paul McKaughan

The world is in constant change. The paradigms and metaphors change as well, but the great unchanging truth that God has given us is His Word—the Bible—our unshakable foundation for life and ministry. Though the foundation may look different through the contextual prism we use to observe it, God's Word remains immutable and infallible.

Global missions has experienced several different emphases in the last half of the 20th century. When I went to the mission field thirty years ago, my focus was on individuals, to win people to Christ. In the 1960s, largely through the influence of Dr. Donald McGavran, church planting became the methodological paradigm, the in thing. Reacting to institutional missions that preceded us, we began to believe that if we could just multiply the number of congregations worldwide that we could accomplish the task of world evangelization. In the mid-1970s Dr. Ralph Winter exposed us to the urgency of reaching those yet unreached people groups—those neglected people groups that had never heard of Jesus. Throughout these transitions the emphasis was on the missionary, as God's primary agent.

Somewhere along the line, many of us began to look back at the great sovereign acts of God. The growth of the Church in Latin

America, the explosive multiplication of the believers in China, or people movements in Africa were not the result of God blessing our plans and our strategies, but rather sovereign acts of God's grace, gathering millions into His kingdom. We discovered that the missionary agent was not necessarily the center of God's strategy to reach the world.

Even those of us who were involved in great strategies, plans, and programs have reluctantly come to the realization that the engineering, strategy-driven model for world evangelization may not be as biblical as we once thought. Yes, we must use good management and developing strategies, but we have discovered that world evangelism starts and ends with Almighty God. Our reductionist definitions of the Great Commission, whether in multiplication of individual conversions or planting multiple churches among every people group on the planet, often have relied on a simplistic reading of the Scriptures.

Spawned in the womb of the industrial revolution, modern missions still lives largely by its dictates—its heroes the engineers, planners and the institution builders. Ours is a "hinge" time where the generational mix in our country and around the world is shifting. It's a wonderful time to look at the future, not to make startling predictions because no one can do that, but rather to try to project present trends into the future. In this kind of projection there will be wild cards which cannot be foreseen and will radically change our projected outcomes, the events in which a sovereign God seems to say, "In spite of your best efforts, I am in control."

What will missions look like ten years from now? While the majority of people, institutions, and technologies that will be with us ten years from now are all present in some form today, the question is, how will these components be configured? If you want evidence of changes just look at the *Fortune 500* list from a few years ago, or even the 100-mega corporations two or three years ago. Most of the forces that will drive missions ten years from now are, likewise, already among us, though they are often unrecognized and their implications misunderstood because we live so much in the past with its traditions and formulas. A wise man once said that *we often drive courageously into the future looking at the world through our rear view mirror.*

The World

The following are some of my assumptions. Some societal trends will continue to drive change, yet there will be many unforeseen turns of events and consequences.

1. Consumerism has become the dominant ideological and economic force around the world.
2. Globalization of commerce, cultural, and educational systems will all continue to be driven by the corporate agendas and the profit motivation.
3. Cutting out middlemen or mediatory institutions. (disintermediation) will accelerate.
4. Transportation, electronic technology, and commerce will continue to drive international integration. The twenty-four/seven, any-time, any-place world will continue to evolve.
5. Countries and geopolitical entities will be squeezed by local, regional, and global concerns and imperatives. In-country wars, rather than global conflagration between super powers, will be the norm.
6. Reactionary revival movements as a quest for individual and corporate meaning will continue. Religion as a force for conflict will largely replace political ideology.
7. Terrorism will continue to disrupt and cause significant anxiety. In the next ten years, there will probably be a thermal nuclear accident or attack.
8. The continued chasm between the rich and the poor, whether for nations or individuals will only increase.
9. Urbanization, driven by technology and consumerism, will continue its unstoppable march.

The Global Church

Any perceptive observer who travels worldwide is immediately impacted by the vitality and sheer size of the Church of Jesus Christ as it has taken root in the Southern Hemisphere and parts of Asia.

Today Christianity is the only true world religion. There are probably more Christians in China than in any country on the planet. One cannot travel in Africa, Latin America or Korea without being aware of the passion and vibrancy of the Christian faith of the people in these regions. This leaves us in the developed West to reflect on the comparative powerlessness and lethargy of our churches, wondering if God has bypassed us.

There is a growing missions commitment by these Southern churches. God is raising up literally tens of thousands of cross-cultural workers from what were "primitive" mission fields a hundred years ago. The world's largest association of mission boards is not in the West, but in India. Nigeria, Brazil, and Korea all send out thousands of cross-cultural missionaries. The continental missionary movement from Latin America is vibrant and growing.

From most of modern missions' history, missions has been from the well-to-do to the poor, the educated to the uneducated. In this emerging movement, missions is a matter of poor people telling other poor people about the grace of God. Cross-cultural missionaries from Africa are going to people groups who have yet to have their first fellowship of believers. They are even sometimes going as illiterates, ministering to people like themselves who cannot read or write.

The new missions movement among the churches where the gospel took root and is flourishing around the world is a mission having to do with demonstration of God's Word, as well as proclamation. For many of these people, God's supernatural works in our time and in our context is something they count on every day.

For them, much of missions is not sending people across the world, but sending members of their own local churches to completely unreached people groups within their homelands and geographical boundaries. They are living out the biblical progression of "Jerusalem . . . and the uttermost." For the future it won't be North Americans or Europeans reaching the unreached people groups of our world, but Latin Americans, Africans and Asians.

These vital churches in the South will increasingly set the agenda and frame the global discussions, theologically as well as methodically. *Ten years from now missions will not be dominated by the missiological engineer of the West, but by the missional artist and poet of the South.*

We American Presbyterians will discover that collaboration with our brothers and sisters from the South will flow out of relationships. Where we once relied on plans and strategies, we will have to become more adept at cross-cultural relationships. This will be time consuming and will necessitate a change in our corporate models, demanding collaborative skills that we don't naturally possess, pushing us well past our problem-solving, entrepreneurial comfort levels.

The last thing I would highlight in this portion is the challenge of growing worldwide Christian nominalism. The growth and zeal of the Church in the Southern Hemisphere is real, but many of these people have no personal relationship to Jesus Christ. In a number of countries, the third generation of the church is in trouble. Like several countries in the West, being a Christian is a social or cultural designation, not a personal commitment, a matter of personal faith. In Korea ministers have told me that if they do not experience a revival, they fear for the vitality of the Church and sustaining of the missions movement in the next ten years. What is our future missional responsibility to a church needing renewal? Global church renewal will become as strategically important as church planting.

What are some of the trends in our own U.S. church that will have an impact on the future? First of all, a grim projection that, apart from a movement of God's Spirit, the missions movement in the U.S. cannot be sustained at its present level.

The boomer generation will not sustain the same level of missional apparatus because they have not bought in to the "missions thing" while the busters may not enjoy the same economic potential and discretionary resources as previous generations. Mission structures must learn to live within more stringent limits, finding that our complex structures and ways of doing missions may be too expensive to maintain. In the global world, the new agencies of the South will increasingly compete for both dollars and personnel.

There will be an increasingly complex missional community. Within the non-profit sector there has been an explosion of new organizations—over one million non-profits registered with the US government. Increasingly missions will be done, utilizing the metaphors of management philosopher, Charles Handy, *(Elephants and Fleas,)* by small entrepreneurial units which are connected largely close to home (fleas) and very large complex organizations that span the globe (elephants).

The local church will be a full partner with mission structures on every level, producing financial and programmatic distress in mission organizations built on the principle of mediation between the distant world and local churches. Frustrated with the large complex structures, many local churches—the elephants—will go it on their own. Disconnected from mission history and practice, many of these new structures will replicate the mistakes of the past, but they will also see many breakthroughs as they experiment and learn. Many other congregations will continue to look to agencies, but on their own terms. The relationship between church and mission will be forged as local churches get involved in the complexities and challenges of cross-cultural ministry far from the home base. Only as churches become involved in the complexities and challenges of cross-cultural ministry will they desire to tap into the reservoir of experience that agencies possess. The question is, Will the agency come alongside to assist the local church in those instances of need?

Short-term missions is here to stay. Short-term missions, however, will be morphing into long-term relationships where individuals, churches and societies go back to the same mission field and forge long-term bonds. Out of short-term missions will evolve many new patterns for a longer-term involvement in God's mission. Mission agencies will have to flex far more than they have in the past if they want to be useful.

A relatively new expression of missionary fervor is becoming known as "Extreme Missions," inspired by the same social context that creates "Extreme Sports." These are movements where young people, mostly singles and married without children, are accepting the dangers of the world in which they live and engaging in missions with "no safety net," going out with a courageous and heroic trust in the God of their fathers. They go out trusting Him for their physical and spiritual safety as they travel to dangerous places.

Bi-vocational ministry will become more prevalent, in which people support themselves financially through the exercise of their specialized vocational skills, at the same time sharing their love for Christ and giving their gifts to local ministry. Whereas this was seen primarily as an access strategy for countries where missionaries were not welcome, for the future it will be an important discipling strategy. Many committed individuals will go into cross-cultural missions work for a period of time during a sabbatical or between jobs.

In this new world of missions, it is becoming increasingly difficult to determine who is the "professional," who is long-term, who is short-term. The terms are going to become meaningless as new models for mission explode across the church and the world.

In this missional world that I have described, there will be the critical need for a corps of cross-cultural career people who will have the relationships and the knowledge of the local church, as well as their own home culture. These men and women will help this shifting missionary force take advantage of high priority opportunities where U.S. personnel can be truly effective on the field for whatever time they can give. They will be the cross-cultural integrators and interpreters that are absolutely essential to long-term effectiveness. They will be the nurturers of coalitions. Only as we are able to form the strategic mix of specialized skills and long-term relationship can we be effective in this 21st century world.

We in the U.S. are a nation of immigrants. Foreign-born, together with the children of foreign-born people, make up about fifty-six million Americans. That's over twenty percent of the population, a fact with a profound implication on our global mission. The 21st century missional church will be the church that is both global and local. The global/local church is the one that reaches out to its own community, recognizing that its people and its commerce link their community to the world. They see these strangers among them as gifts from God, a part of God's strategy to reach a world that has yet to hear the good news of Jesus Christ. These individuals regularly visit friends, families, and colleagues back home who need to experience God's grace. We must have more and more of these people in our churches because our churches must be congruent in their local, national, and international vision and outreach. The discontinuity between the "foreign" and "home" ministry of the church, so prevalent in missions, must be eradicated. In so doing, it is essential that the local church maintain its outward focus, rather than following its tendency to inward focus, failing to remember that God brought them into existence for His glory among the nations and not for themselves.

Lastly, we live in a world in which the vitality of the church, its scholarship and wisdom has moved decisively south. The missional driving force today comes from the Two-Thirds World churches our own movements produced. Our emphasis on direct church planting will probably give way to a ministry of facilitation and support of those efforts. The rediscovery of our responsibility to plant vital congregations was a wonderful corrective to a more institutional missions movement fifty years ago. But now is the time to rediscover the whole counsel of God and to involve ourselves in partnership with national movements around the world that will seek to truly impact their people with the power and vitality of the good news of Jesus Christ. In this context, institutions may emerge and must be nurtured, but the initiative for those programs must spring from the local context of ministry. Support structures for the church must be both desperately needed and economically viable in the local context. The growth of the church is our calling, but in the future some of our simplistic and reductionist definitions of this must give way to a more complete understanding of Christ's kingdom. The mere multiplication of congregations, though an important indicator of the health of the church, must have the impact of salt and light in the society in which she is planted. Our missional vision must include these fuller definitions.

What Now?

How do we as a church interact with what God is doing in the world? I don't believe we should fight the context or look back longingly at the good old days. We must look to the future. Acting right starts with thinking right. Appropriate response starts with God, His Word, and an appropriate application of its truths in our culture at home and globally. His Holy Spirit will apply His Word and burden our heart with vision for the future. We must recognize that the sovereign Lord has given His church this time and this place to proclaim and live out kingdom values.

Secondly, look for opportunities in the new global/local context. We often spend time in lamentation, when we should be looking for future opportunities. God's biblical promises were not limited to the past. They have application for today and tomorrow. Crisis times are often the times of greatest opportunity. Problems cry out for solutions, and questions need answers.

Thirdly, look at the resources that God has placed at your disposal. The deployment of that which God has given us can be multiplied when used to exploit God-given opportunities. Lamenting what God has not placed at our disposal merely paralyzes us. Someone once told me that, if you want to know what God means to do, look first to see who (the skills and gifts) God has brought to you. God will rarely give us additional resources when we are not exercising good stewardship over what we have. As we look at what God is doing around the world, how can we apply those resources to work with great movements of God's Spirit that are exploding across the globe?

*Rev. **Paul McKaughan** is president of the Evangelical Fellowship of Mission Agencies and previously served as Coordinator of Mission to the World. He and his wife, Joanne, served eighteen years in Brazil and thirty-six years in international missions.*

For Further Reading and Study

1. *A Mind for Missions,* Paul Borthwick, Navpress, November 1987
2. *The Call: Finding and Fulfilling the Central Purpose of Your Life*, Os Guinness, Word Publishing, May 1998
3. Cities: Mission's New Frontier, Roger Greenway and Timothy Monsma, Baker Book House, May 2000
4. *Eternity in Their Hearts*, Don Richardson, Regal Books, May 1984
5. *Evangelism: Doing Justice and Preaching Grace*, Harvie Conn, Presbyterian and Reformed Publishing Company, July 1992
6. *From Jerusalem to Irian Jaya*, Ruth Tucker, Zondervan Publishing Company, September 1983
7. *Go and Make Disciples! An Introduction to Christian Missions*, Roger Greenway, Presbyterian and Reformed Publishing Company, October 1999
8. *The Great Omission,* Robertson McQuilken, Gabriel Publishing, March 2002
9. *He Gave Us a Valley*, Helen Roseveare, Intervarsity Press, June 1976
10. *Hudson Taylor's Spiritual Secret,* Dr. and Mrs. Hudson Taylor, Moody Press, December 1987
11. *Let the Nations Be Glad*, John Piper, Baker Book House, August 1993
12. *Ministering Cross-Culturally*, Sherwood Lingenfelter and Marvin Mayers, Baker Book House, September 1986
13. *Ministries of Mercy: The Call of the Jericho Road*, Tim Keller, 2nd Edition, Presbyterian and Reformed Publishing Company, August 1997

14. *Missionary Methods: St. Paul's or Ours*, Roland Allen, Wm. B. Eerdmans Publishing Company, June 1962

15. *Muslims and Christians at the Table*, Bruce McDowell and Anees Zaka, Presbyterian and Reformed Publishing Company, October 1999

16. *Mustard Seed Vs. McWorld: Reinventing Life and Faith for the Future*, Tom Sine, Baker Book House, August 1999

17. *The Open Secret: An Introduction to the Theology of Mission*, Lesslie Newbigin, Wm. B. Eerdmans Publishing Company, February 1995

18. *Operation World: When We Pray God Works*, Patrick Johnstone and Jason Mandryk, Paternoster Publishing, September 2001

19. *Perspectives on the World Christian Movement, A Reader*, Ralph Winter and Steven Hawthorne, Gabriel Resources, July 1992

20. *Reaching Muslims for Christ*, William Saal, Moody Press, February 1993

21. *Serving As Senders*, Neal Pirolo, Emmaus Road International, August 1991

22. *Shadow of the Almighty*, Elisabeth Elliot, Harper San Francisco, July 1989

23. *Toward a Theology of Movement*, Gary Waldecker (summary version, available only from Mission to the World)

24. *Transforming Mission: Paradigm Shifts in Theology of Mission*, David Bosch, Orbis Books, April 1991

25. *Window on the World*, Daphne Spruggett, Authentic Media, May 2002

For more information about

Mission to the World

please contact us or visit our web site.

Mission to the World
1600 North Brown Road
Lawrenceville, GA 30043-8141
phone: 678 823 0004
email: info@mtw.org
www.mtw.org